Project Management Institute

PRACTICE STANDARD FOR
EARNED VALUE MANAGEMENT

Second Edition

D1441802

Library of Congress Cataloging-in-Publication Data

Practice standard for earned value management / Project Management
Institute. -- 2nd ed.
      p. cm.
  Includes bibliographical references and index.
  ISBN 978-1-935589-35-8 (pbk. : alk. paper) 1. Project
management--Standards. I. Project Management Institute.
  HD69.P75P65155 2011
  658.4'04--dc23

                              2011035062

Published by:
  Project Management Institute, Inc.
  14 Campus Boulevard
  Newtown Square, Pennsylvania 19073-3299 USA.
  Phone: +610-356-4600
  Fax: +610-356-4647
  E-mail: customercare@pmi.org
  Internet: www.PMI.org

©2011 Project Management Institute, Inc. All rights reserved.

"PMI", the PMI logo, "PMP", the PMP logo, "PMBOK", "PgMP", "Project Management Journal", "PM Network", and the PMI Today logo are registered marks of Project Management Institute, Inc. The Quarter Globe Design is a trademark of the Project Management Institute, Inc. For a comprehensive list of PMI marks, contact the PMI Legal Department.

PMI Publications welcomes corrections and comments on its books. Please feel free to send comments on typographical, formatting, or other errors. Simply make a copy of the relevant page of the book, mark the error, and send it to: Book Editor, PMI Publications, 14 Campus Boulevard, Newtown Square, PA 19073-3299 USA.

To inquire about discounts for resale or educational purposes, please contact the PMI Book Service Center.
  PMI Book Service Center
  P.O. Box 932683, Atlanta, GA 31193-2683 USA
  Phone: 1-866-276-4764 (within the U.S. or Canada) or +1-770-280-4129 (globally)
  Fax: +1-770-280-4113
  E-mail: info@bookorders.pmi.org

Printed in the United States of America. No part of this work may be reproduced or transmitted in any form or by any means, electronic, manual, photocopying, recording, or by any information storage and retrieval system, without prior written permission of the publisher.

The paper used in this book complies with the Permanent Paper Standard issued by the National Information Standards Organization (Z39.48—1984).

10 9 8 7 6 5 4 3 2

NOTICE

The Project Management Institute, Inc. (PMI) standards and guideline publications, of which the document contained herein is one, are developed through a voluntary consensus standards development process. This process brings together volunteers and/or seeks out the views of persons who have an interest in the topic covered by this publication. While PMI administers the process and establishes rules to promote fairness in the development of consensus, it does not write the document and it does not independently test, evaluate, or verify the accuracy or completeness of any information or the soundness of any judgments contained in its standards and guideline publications.

PMI disclaims liability for any personal injury, property or other damages of any nature whatsoever, whether special, indirect, consequential or compensatory, directly or indirectly resulting from the publication, use of application, or reliance on this document. PMI disclaims and makes no guaranty or warranty, expressed or implied, as to the accuracy or completeness of any information published herein, and disclaims and makes no warranty that the information in this document will fulfill any of your particular purposes or needs. PMI does not undertake to guarantee the performance of any individual manufacturer or seller's products or services by virtue of this standard or guide.

In publishing and making this document available, PMI is not undertaking to render professional or other services for or on behalf of any person or entity, nor is PMI undertaking to perform any duty owed by any person or entity to someone else. Anyone using this document should rely on his or her own independent judgment or, as appropriate, seek the advice of a competent professional in determining the exercise of reasonable care in any given circumstances. Information and other standards on the topic covered by this publication may be available from other sources, which the user may wish to consult for additional views or information not covered by this publication.

PMI has no power, nor does it undertake to police or enforce compliance with the contents of this document. PMI does not certify, test, or inspect products, designs, or installations for safety or health purposes. Any certification or other statement of compliance with any health or safety-related information in this document shall not be attributable to PMI and is solely the responsibility of the certifier or maker of the statement.

TABLE OF CONTENTS

PREFACE

The *Practice Standard for Earned Value Management*—Second Edition is a complement to *A Guide to the Project Management Body of Knowledge* (*PMBOK® Guide*).

In April 2010, Dr. Lingguang Song of the University of Houston released the results of a comprehensive PMI College of Performance Management (as the PMI EVM Community of Practice was then known) funded research survey managed by the PMI Research Foundation. This research comprehensively examined the global practice of earned value management (EVM) with the findings published in a book entitled *Earned Value Management: A Global and Cross-industry Perspective on Current EVM Practice*.

In that study one of the many important conclusions was that "EVM's contributions and cost effectiveness are widely recognized by all users regardless of their industry sector, motivation, and country." Other significant findings include EVM users in general "agree" to "strongly agree" with EVM's contributions to providing early warning, helping to achieve cost goals, improving communication, helping to achieve schedule goals, and improving scope management. Dr Song's research also concluded, based on a sample size of over 700 respondents that the *Practice Standard for Earned Value Management* is the most widely used and influential standard in the global EVM community.

This second edition of the practice standard expands greatly on the foundation established by the previous edition by implementing a process approach to assist in understanding and application of earned value management.

The overarching goal of this practice standard is to facilitate improvement in project performance outcomes by encouraging the use of EVM on projects. The intent is to expand upon the concept of EVM as presented in the *PMBOK® Guide* in a way that allows for easy understanding and implementation.

The *Practice Standard for Earned Value Management* is organized into the following chapters:

- **Introduction**.
- **Earned Value Management Overview**—outlines the basic principles and concepts of earned value management.
- **Organize Project**—covers the process of developing a detailed description of the project and explains the importance of the work breakdown structure (WBS), the WBS dictionary, and the scope baseline.
- **Assign Responsibility**—explains the importance of identifying the individuals responsible for all aspects of project execution.
- **Develop Schedule**—provides a brief treatment of the project schedule and is the first document that measures all of the work that constitutes the project scope. This chapter also covers the schedule baseline.

- **Establish Budget**—covers the natural extension of the schedule baseline into a cost baseline. Includes cost estimating, work authorization, and the project budget log.

- **Determine Measurement Methods**—describes the processes and considerations of choosing the appropriate earned value measurement technique for determining earned value (EV). This chapter includes an explanation of the three classes of work (discrete, apportioned, and level of effort).

- **Establish the Performance Measurement Baseline**—covers the process of integrating the scope, schedule, and cost baselines into a single project baseline to manage, measure, and control project performance throughout execution. This chapter also covers the contingency and management reserves, undistributed budget, and rolling wave planning.

- **Analyze Project Performance**—explains how to use the outputs of an earned value management system to assess and forecast project cost and schedule performance. This is the longest chapter in the practice standard and includes a thorough coverage of the EVM metrics, including the graphical presentation of EVM data plus a tutorial on the meaning of the various EVM metrics and predictors.

- **Maintain Performance Measurement Baseline**—describes the process of managing changes to the project scope and maintaining the integrity of the performance measurement baseline.

In addition to the ten chapters that cover the core concepts of EVM, there are three appendices that have been written for the purpose of bringing additional insight to some of the specialized and topical areas with EVM:

- **Appendix D—Schedule Analysis Using Earned Value Data**

- **Appendix E—Integrating Earned Value Management with Risk Management**

- **Appendix F—Deployment of Earned Value Management Systems**

- **Appendix G—Pitfalls and Recommendations**

Throughout this practice standard we used a "single thread example" of a bicycle project to illustrate and explain the concepts and application of the Earned value method. This model of building a bicycle was utilized from the start to illustrate the development of the WBS all the way through to the final chapter where it is used to demonstrate the impact of changes to the project's cost and schedule baselines.

This practice standard is consistent with the *PMBOK® Guide*. It was developed with the global project management community in mind with the intent that the EVM concepts presented are applicable to projects of various sizes and complexity in a broad scope of industries in the government, commercial and nongovernment organization sectors.

The Project Management Institute's standards program will continue to periodically update this standard as part of the overall planned evolution of PMI standards. Comments from project management practitioners are both requested and welcome.

CHAPTER 1

INTRODUCTION

The *Practice Standard for Earned Value Management*—Second Edition has been developed as a supplement to *A Guide to the Project Management Body of Knowledge (PMBOK® Guide)* [1].[1] A practice standard is a document that describes established norms, methods, processes, and practices. The information in this practice standard evolved from the recognized good practices of earned value management (EVM) project management practitioners. It reflects what are considered to be best practices on projects that use earned value management techniques. The practice standard provides guidelines for managing individual projects. It does not provide information on managing programs or portfolios of projects.

This practice standard is designed to provide readers who are familiar with the fundamental practices of project management, as outlined in the *PMBOK® Guide*, with a practical understanding of the principles of EVM and its role in facilitating effective project management.

This is the second edition of this practice standard and builds on the work from the previous edition. It expands on many of the concepts and provides information about the infrastructure and processes necessary to conduct earned value management effectively. The second edition is completely reformatted to follow a process orientation.

1.1 Purpose of this Practice Standard

The *Practice Standard for Earned Valued Management* identifies a subset of project management practices that are used for earned value management.

The *Practice Standard for Earned Value Management* also promotes a common vocabulary. The definitions of key terms are aligned with the *Lexicon*, although not all vocabulary and definitions used in this practice standard are in the *Lexicon*.

This practice standard is not intended to be all-inclusive. There are many different methodologies and tools for implementing the processes described in this practice standard.

---

[1] The **boldface** numbers in brackets refer to the list of references at the end of this practice standard.

1.2 Relationship to the *PMBOK® Guide*

The *Practice Standard for Earned Value Management* focuses on the effective integration of those project management practices that are used for earned value management. It does not reiterate information in the *PMBOK® Guide*. For purposes of this practice standard, it is assumed that a project has been initiated following the processes outlined in the Initiating Process Group defined in the *PMBOK® Guide*. As such, it is assumed that high-level requirements documentation has been gathered along with other information in the project charter, stakeholders have been identified, and a strategy to manage their requirements and expectations has been developed.

The *PMBOK® Guide* identifies a set of internal and external environmental factors, called enterprise environmental factors, which may influence a project's success. They may enhance or constrain project management options and they may have a positive or negative influence on the outcomes. Examples of these include:

- Organizational culture, structure, and processes
- Government or industry standards
- Infrastructure
- Company work authorization systems
- Project management information systems

The previous list is not complete, but it provides an example of those factors that can positively or negatively influence projects that use EVM. For a more robust list, refer to the *PMBOK® Guide*.

In addition to enterprise environmental factors, the *PMBOK® Guide* also defines organizational process assets. These include policies, procedures, templates, forms, knowledge bases, and information from previous projects that can have an influence on project success. There are two main categories: (1) processes and procedures and (2) the corporate knowledge base. The following is an abbreviated list (refer to the *PMBOK® Guide* for a more complete list).

- Processes and procedures
- Standard project life cycles
- Policies
- Templates
- Financial control procedures
- Change control procedures
- Work authorization procedures
- Corporate knowledge base
- Project files

- Lessons learned

- Historical information from past projects

- Estimating information from past projects

Enterprise environmental factors and organizational process assets are inputs to almost every process. They are explicitly listed in the *PMBOK® Guide.* However, the *Practice Standard for Earned Value Management* will not list them as inputs, although you can assume they are present. In certain instances a specific item will be identified, for example, work authorization procedures can be presented as an input if appropriate.

1.3 Assumptions

While the basic concept of EVM can and perhaps should be applied on every project where resource management and cost/schedule outcomes are important, this practice standard presents information for implementation on a large project. Additional assumptions include:

- The organization has the corporate policies and procedures to support EVM.

- The organization has the integrated information systems necessary to implement EVM.

- The project management team has the knowledge and skills needed to plan, execute, and control projects using EVM.

- Project team members and other stakeholders have sufficient training and understanding of EVM concepts to plan their work accordingly.

1.4 Structure of the Practice Standard

This practice standard has ten chapters. This first chapter is an introduction. Chapter 2 provides a high-level overview of EVM. The remaining chapters present a process perspective for planning, executing, and controlling project work using EVM.

Chapters 3 through 10 follow a similar format as outlined below.

- **Introduction.** Introduces the concept that will be described in the chapter. Includes a graphic with inputs and outputs.

- **Inputs.** Identifies the documents necessary to conduct the process.

- **Description.** Describes the methods, tools, and techniques used to conduct the process.

- **Outputs.** Identifies the documents or outcomes that are a result of the process.

- **Considerations.** Discusses variables and perspectives that an EVM practitioner needs to keep in mind when implementing the process.

- **Summary.** Summarizes the information in the chapter.

CHAPTER 2

EARNED VALUE PROJECT MANAGEMENT OVERVIEW

2.1 Introduction

The *Practice Standard for Earned Value Management* was developed as a supplement to *A Guide to the Project Management Body of Knowledge (PMBOK® Guide)*. The purpose of this practice standard is to:

- Provide a standard for project management practitioners and other stakeholders that defines the essential aspects of applying earned value in project management.

- Provide a reference for the basic concepts and applications of earned value management that is consistent and globally applicable.

Earned value management is a management methodology for integrating scope, schedule, and resources; for objectively measuring project performance and progress; and for forecasting project outcome. The application of earned value in the early initiation and planning phases of a project increases the validity and usefulness of the cost and schedule baseline and is an excellent verification of the project scope assumptions and the scope baseline. Once established, these baselines become the best source for understanding project performance during execution. A comparison of actual performance (both cost and schedule) against this baseline provides feedback on project status and data, not only for projecting probable outcomes, but also for management to make timely and useful decisions using objective data.

A fundamental principle of EVM is that patterns and trends of performance, when compared against a soundly developed baseline, can be excellent predictors of the future project performance. Feedback is critical to the success of any project. Timely and targeted feedback can enable project managers to identify problems early and make adjustments that can keep a project on time and on budget. EVM is considered by many to be one of the most effective performance measurement and feedback tools for managing projects.

In addition to basic cost and schedule baseline development and performance feedback, EVM also emphasizes the importance of many other considerations necessary for project management, such as organizational structure, cost collection strategies, and the incorporation of approved project changes.

EVM provides organizations with the methodology needed to integrate the management of project scope, schedule, and resources. This standard uses the term project scope to mean the work that must be performed to deliver a product, service or result with the specified features and functions. EVM can play a crucial role in answering management questions that are critical to the success of every project, such as:

- Are we delivering more or less work than planned?

- When is the project likely to be completed?

- Are we currently over or under budget?

- What is the remaining work likely to cost?

- What is the entire project likely to cost?
- How much will we be over or under budget at the end of the project?
- What is driving the significant cost and/or schedule variances?

2.2 EVM and the Project Management Process

The practice of EVM is consistent with good project management as outlined in *A Guide to the Project Management Body of Knowledge* (*PMBOK® Guide*). Figure 2-1 shows the relationship between EVM and the *PMBOK® Guide's* Project Management Process Groups and Knowledge Areas, and highlights the areas of project management to which EVM is fundamentally most applicable.

Project planning is mostly a matter of determining:

- What work must be done (scope) and in what pieces (work breakdown structure).
- Who is going to perform and manage the work (responsibility assignment matrix).
- When the work will be done (schedule).
- The cost and quantity of the labor, material, and related resources the work will require.

Knowledge Areas	Process Groups				
	Initiating	Planning	Executing	Monitoring & Controlling	Closing
Project Integration Management	X	X	X	X	X
Project Scope Management		X		X	
Project Time Management		X		X	
Project Cost Management		X		X	
Project Quality Management		X	X	X	
Project Human Resource Management		X	X		
Project Communications Management		X	X	X	
Project Risk Management		X		X	
Project Procurement Management		X	X	X	X

LEGEND

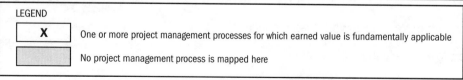

X	One or more project management processes for which earned value is fundamentally applicable
	No project management process is mapped here

Figure 2-1. EVM and Project Management

Practice Standard for Earned Value Management — Second Edition
©2011 Project Management Institute, 14 Campus Blvd., Newtown Square, PA 19073-3299 USA

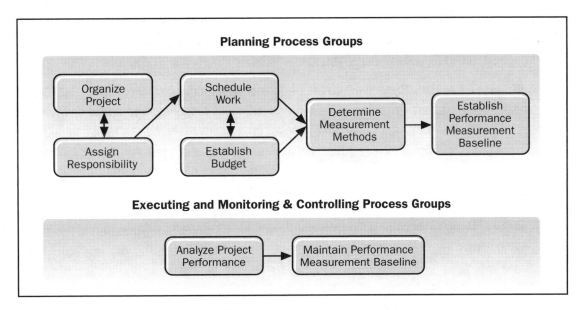

Figure 2-2. The Earned Value Management Process

Project control focuses mostly on monitoring and reporting the execution of project management plans. Project control is a process for keeping work performance and results within a specified tolerance range of the work plan.

As a performance management methodology, EVM adds some critical practices to the project management process. These practices occur primarily in the areas of project planning, execution, and control, and are related to the goal of measuring, analyzing, forecasting, and reporting cost and schedule performance data for evaluation and action by the project team and other key stakeholders.

The structure of this *Practice Standard for Earned Value Management* will focus on these processes. For purposes of this practice standard, it is assumed that a project has been initiated, stakeholders have been identified, and the project and product requirements have been collected. Therefore, this practice standard begins with defining the scope after the requirements have been defined. Figure 2-2 illustrates the process flow that will be used to introduce the EVM topics discussed in this practice standard.

2.3 Basic EVM Terminology

Throughout this practice standard, core terminology is used frequently and is fairly unique to earned value management. These terms are defined in greater detail in later chapters; however, an overview in this chapter may help with a basic understanding of this practice standard.

- **Actual Cost (AC).** The realized cost incurred for the work performed on an activity during a specific time period. This can be reported for cumulative to date or for a specific reporting period. May also be known as the actual cost of work performed (ACWP).

- **Budget at Completion (BAC).** The sum of all the budgets established for the work to be performed on a project, work breakdown structure component, control account, or work package. The project BAC is the sum of all work package BACs.

- **Contingency Reserve.** Budget within the performance management baseline that is allocated for identified risks that are accepted or for which contingent responses are devised. While not often used on ANSI-748-compliant projects [2], these contingency reserves can fund contingency plans, fall back plans, or address the residual risk that remains after the risk response planning process. Unlike management reserve, which is not in the performance measurement baseline (PMB) but is a part of the project budget base (PBB), contingency reserves are considered to be within the PMB. In commercial environments, the explicit use of contingency reserves in the EVM method is quite common. In more traditional and government-based EVM environments, the only budget within the PMB that is outside of the WBS and is not time-phased is the undistributed budget (UB). In this case, contingency reserve can be treated as a special application of UB with the difference that it will only be distributed when a risk occurs or a contingency plan is implemented. Because contingency reserve is a budget within the PMB that may be without identifiable scope, the application of contingency reserves on projects with an ANSI-748 compliance requirement may not be acceptable.

- **Control Account.** A management control point where scope, budget, actual cost, and schedule are integrated and compared to earned value for performance measurement. Each control account may be further decomposed into work packages and/or planning packages. Control accounts can belong to only one WBS component and one organizational breakdown component.

- **Distributed Budget.** The budget for project scope that has been identified to work breakdown structure (WBS) control accounts. This budget also has an identified responsible manager (control account manager). The distributed budget forms the basis for the planned value (PV).

- **Earned Value (EV).** The measure of the work performed, expressed in terms of the budget authorized for that work. Earned value can be reported for cumulative to date or for a specific reporting period. May also be known as the budgeted cost for work performed (BCWP).

- **Estimate at Completion (EAC).** The expected total cost of completing all work expressed as the sum of the actual cost to date and the estimate to complete (ETC).

- **Estimate To Complete (ETC).** The estimated cost to finish all the remaining work. Adding the ETC to the actual cost (AC) will result in the estimate at completion (EAC) at any level of the project.

- **Management Reserve (MR).** An amount of the project budget base (PBB) withheld for management control purposes. These are budgets reserved for unforeseen work that is within scope of the project. The use of management reserve requires special authorization from management. It is used in special circumstances where the project manager sees the need to change the performance measurement baseline, but doesn't change the project's budget as defined in the contract or project charter.

- **Performance Measurement Baseline (PMB).** An approved integrated scope-schedule-cost plan for the project work against which project execution is compared to measure and manage performance.

The PMB is formed by the budgets assigned to control accounts plus budgets with identified scope that have not been distributed to control accounts (undistributed budget). The PMB is the equal to the distributed budget plus the undistributed budget. It does not include management reserve.

- **Planned Value (PV).** The authorized budget assigned to scheduled work as of a given reporting date. At any point in time, planned value defines the work that should have been accomplished. Planned value can be reported for cumulative work to date or for a specific reporting period. May also be known as the budgeted cost for work scheduled.

- **Planning Package.** Work and budget that have been identified to a control account but are not yet defined into work packages. This is a future effort for which detailed planning may not have been accomplished. Prior to beginning the effort within a planning package, work and budget must first be converted to one or more work packages.

- **Project Budget Base (PBB).** The starting point upon which original budgets are built. This represents the total budget for the project, including any management reserve and estimated costs for work that has been authorized but is not yet fully defined. When the project is chartered by a contract, this is known as the contract budget base (CBB).

- **Summary Level Planning Budget (SLPB).** A time-phased budget for future work that cannot be reasonably planned down to control accounts. Budget and scope held in SLPB should be moved to control accounts as soon as practicable, but before the work within them begins. Not all projects will use an SLPB, but it is an available tool in certain circumstances. May also be known as a summary level planning package (SLPP).

- **Undistributed Budget (UB).** The budget for project scope that has not yet been identified to WBS elements and, below those, to control accounts. This budget has not yet been distributed to a responsible control account manager (CAM). An undistributed budget is generally not time-phased.

- **Work Package.** The work defined at the lowest level of the work breakdown structure for which cost and duration can be estimated and managed. Each work package has a unique scope of work, budget, scheduled start and completion dates, and may only belong to one control account.

- **Work Breakdown Structure (WBS).** The work breakdown structure (WBS) is a hierarchical decomposition of the total scope of the work to be carried out by the project team to accomplish the project objectives to create the required deliverables. For EVM, the work breakdown structure is a deliverable-oriented hierarchical decomposition of the work to be executed by the project team in order to accomplish the project objectives. It organizes and defines the total scope of the project. See the *Practice Standard for Work Breakdown Structures* [3] for additional information.

- **Work Breakdown Structure Dictionary.** A document that provides detailed deliverable, activity, and scheduling information about each component in the work breakdown structure. See the *Practice Standard for Work Breakdown Structures* for additional information.

Figure 2-3 shows a sample chart that depicts many of these terms. Another depiction of the relationship between the budget elements is illustrated in Figure 2-4.

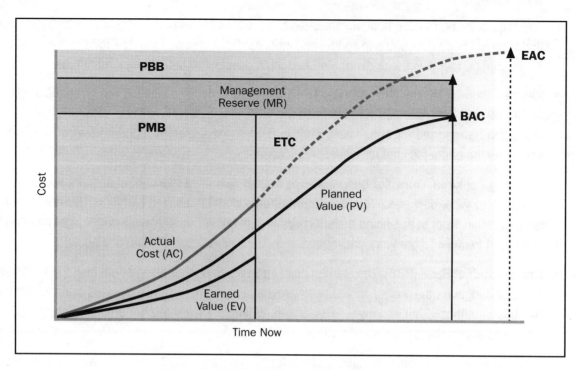

Figure 2-3. EVM Basic Concepts: Chart Form

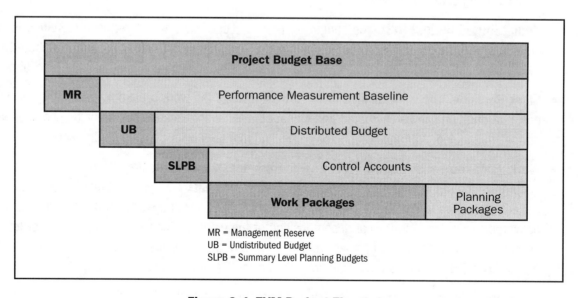

MR = Management Reserve
UB = Undistributed Budget
SLPB = Summary Level Planning Budgets

Figure 2-4. EVM Budget Elements

2.4 Basic EVM Concepts

Proper planning requires *a firm grasp of product and project scope.* During the planning process, emphasis is placed on gaining agreement among the key stakeholders regarding the project objectives. At this point, the scope of the project needs to be further elaborated, using a work breakdown structure, into executable and manageable elements called work packages. The work packages are organized in control accounts according to the project organization breakdown structure and responsibility assignment matrix. The control account manager is responsible for detailed planning of work packages within their control account.

Project work needs to be logically scheduled through the completion of the project, including the identification of critical milestones. The project schedule will show the timing of key accomplishments and interfaces, plus provide evidence that the project management plan supports the stakeholder agreement regarding project objectives. Scheduling cannot be executed without knowledge of resource availability and constraints. This is an iterative process until a balance is struck that meets project scheduling objectives within the identified resource limitations.

Once the work is logically scheduled and resources identified, the work scope, schedule, and cost need to be integrated and recorded in a time-phased budget known as the performance measurement baseline. This is the time-phased budget plan that will be used to measure project performance. In the planning process, the means for assessing physical work progress and assigning earned value is documented. In addition to routine project management planning, earned value measurement techniques are selected and applied for each work package based on scope, schedule, and cost considerations.

In the project execution process, EVM requires the recording of resource utilization (i.e., labor, materials, and the like) for the work performed within each of the work elements in the project management plan. In other words, actual costs need to be captured in such a way (both per the WBS and the calendar) that permits their comparison with the performance measurement baseline. Actual costs are collected at the control account level or below.

In the project control process, EVM requires physical work progress assessment and assessing earned value (using the selected earned value measurement methods). With this earned value (EV) data, the planned value (PV) data from the performance measurement baseline, and the actual cost (AC) data from the project cost tracking system, the project team can perform EVM analysis at the control account and other levels of the project work breakdown structure and report the EVM results as needed. In addition, this analysis can be used to develop corrective action plans for any discovered issues and update the forecast of expected project costs.

Project changes, either driven by stakeholders external to the project team or by the project team themselves, are implemented into the project baseline in a timely and accurate fashion using a change control system established for the program. The same care that was taken to initially establish the performance measurement baseline (PMB) needs to be continued to maintain a valid PMB throughout the life of the project.

In summary, EVM facilitates the planning and control of cost and schedule performance, thus improving project management visibility and understanding. The key practices of EVM for planning, executing, and controlling a project include:

1. Define product and project scope and decompose work to a manageable level.
2. Assign clear management responsibility for discrete work elements.

3. Plan the activities of the project into a logical schedule.
4. Develop a time-phased budget for each element of the WBS.
5. Select EV measurement techniques for each work package prior to execution.
6. Establish a performance measurement baseline based on the previous five steps.
7. Develop a structure for collecting costs into the same accounts and time periods where performance is being measured.
8. Determine earned value by objectively measuring the physical work progress according to the earned value technique selected for the work.
9. Analyze cost/schedule performance.
10. Forecast cost /schedule performance.
11. Project the estimates at completion.
12. Report performance problems and take appropriate corrective action.
13. Maintain integrity of the PMB.

2.5 Considerations

While this practice standard assumes the implementation of EVM on a large project in order to provide all necessary information on EVM, this practice standard may be applicable to smaller scale projects as well. EVM is scalable, and implementing the approach depicted in the EVM system diagram in Figure 2-5 enables the basic concept of EVM to be implemented on projects of any size.

Alignment of the activities defined in the WBS into the project cost and scheduling subsystems is a project management practice. This also enables the project to undertake the following EVM core concepts:

- Measuring and comparing the value of the work performed (earned value) with the value planned and actual costs expended to accomplish that work as the project progresses.

- Developing forecasts, for example, EAC, ETC, VAC, etc.

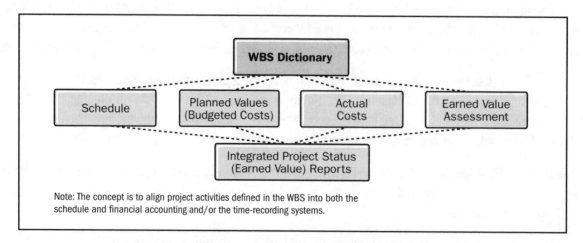

Figure 2-5. EVM System Diagram (Source: *Earned Schedule* **[4]**).

CHAPTER 3

ORGANIZE PROJECT

3.1 Introduction

Organize Project is the process of developing a detailed description of the project and products subdividing the project deliverables into a hierarchy of defined work packages.

Project management depends on understanding and planning the project's goals and objectives. One of the first steps in planning a project is defining the scope. This chapter provides a process to define the project scope and discusses the key elements that comprise that process. Inputs and outputs are provided in Figure 3-1.

3.2 Inputs

3.2.1 Project Charter

The project charter is a document issued by the project initiator or sponsor that formally authorizes the existence of a project and provides a project manager with the authority to apply organizational resources to project activities. The project charter provides the high-level project requirements and high-level product or service description of the project. It establishes a partnership between the performing organization and the requesting organization or customer. The approved project charter includes information from a signed contract if one exists. The charter formally initiates the project. The charter gives the project manager the authority to apply organizational resources to accomplish the objectives of the project. The project charter typically contains the project purpose, the objectives, and related success criteria, high-level requirements, project description and risks, as well as a budget estimate and critical milestone schedule. For purposes of this standard we will assume the charter incorporates relevant information from a customer contract.

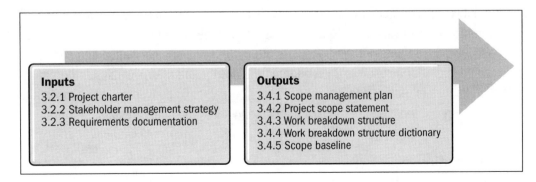

Inputs
3.2.1 Project charter
3.2.2 Stakeholder management strategy
3.2.3 Requirements documentation

Outputs
3.4.1 Scope management plan
3.4.2 Project scope statement
3.4.3 Work breakdown structure
3.4.4 Work breakdown structure dictionary
3.4.5 Scope baseline

Figure 3-1. Organize Project: Inputs and Outputs

3.2.2 Stakeholder Management Strategy

The stakeholder management strategy is designed to engage the project stakeholders in the success of the project. For each stakeholder, it includes areas of interest, type and degree of influence on the project, and strategies to increase support for the project.

3.2.3 Requirements Documentation

After the charter is approved or the contract is signed, the high-level requirements are further decomposed and documented. Stakeholder needs are refined into project requirements and product and/or service requirements. Product/service requirements define the features and functions that describe a product, service, or result and include information on technical requirements, security requirements, performance requirements, etc. The project requirements include information on business requirements, project management requirements, delivery requirements, etc. In other words, the requirements documentation defines the condition or capability that must be present in a product, service, or result to satisfy a contract or other formally proposed specification.

3.3 Description

3.3.1 Product Analysis

Product analysis is a method used to translate product and/or service descriptions and requirements into deliverables. A cross-functional group of stakeholders takes information about the features and functions and determines the deliverables and components necessary to meet the product or service requirements.

3.3.2 Alternatives Analysis

Alternatives analysis is used to ensure the best approach for meeting project objectives and stakeholder requirements. There are numerous solutions or approaches to accomplishing any given project. Performing cost, schedule, and performance analysis on each of these alternatives will help to better define the most efficient and effective solution to meet the stakeholder's expectations. This analysis needs to be thorough and take into consideration the expected performance and associated risks of the product or service, the cost to develop it, produce it, and maintain it throughout its life cycle. For each alternative, the cost-benefit trade-off and the effectiveness of that solution is documented. Without the alternative analysis, the chosen alternative may meet the stakeholders' end needs, but may not be affordable. Or conversely, the chosen alternative may be affordable, but may not meet one or more of the stakeholders' end needs/results.

3.3.3 Decomposition

Decomposition starts with the end deliverables and continuously breaks them into smaller components. The upper levels typically reflect the major deliverable work areas of the project or major phases in the project's life cycle. The content of the upper levels may vary, depending upon the type of project and the industry involved. These levels provide logical summary points for assessing team and individual performance, communicating accomplishments, and measuring cost and schedule performance with respect to individual deliverables as well as the overall project.

The upper levels of the WBS are normally used for reporting purposes. The lower-level WBS elements provide appropriate focus for project management processes such as scope and schedule development, cost estimating and budgeting, and risk assessment. The translation of the requirements necessary to meet the needs of the principal stakeholders into the WBS essentially forms the scope of the project. The WBS becomes the centralized structure for the communication of project information. Figure 3-2 provides an example.

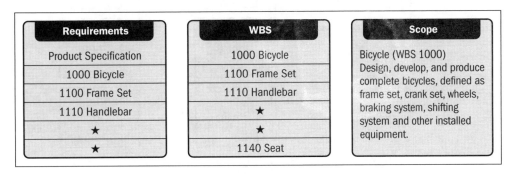

Figure 3-2. Integrating Requirements with Work Activities

The WBS divides the project scope into hierarchical, manageable, definable elements of work that balance the control needs of management with an appropriate and effective level of detailed project data. The various levels of the WBS also provide support for focusing communication with stakeholders and aid in clearly identifying accountability to a level of detail necessary for the effective management and control of the project.

The WBS includes all of the work defined by the project scope and captures all deliverables—internal, external, and interim—including project management. The WBS is structured on the concept of "parent" and "child" relationships (see Figure 3-3). That is, the next lower-level elements of detail for any single WBS element are referred to as the "children" of the "parent" WBS element. Thus, no "child" element of the WBS can summarize into more than one "parent" element. The sum of the work contained within a "parent's children" must equal 100% of the work of the "parent."

Figure 3-4 is a sample WBS designed to capture the scope of work required to construct a bicycle. To keep the graphic simple, this particular WBS assumes that the detailed requirements for a specific type of bicycle would be provided as further decompositions of the illustrated WBS elements. This example of a project to build a bicycle will be used throughout the standard to demonstrate the principles introduced in the remaining chapters.

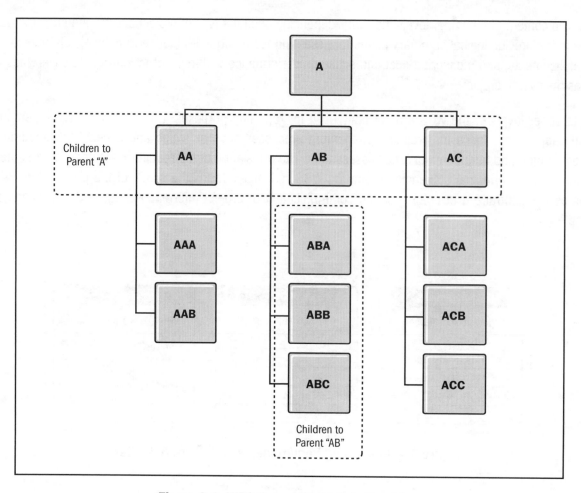

Figure 3-3. WBS Parent/Child Relationships

Specifically, this example illustrates each element of work, the various levels of a WBS, and the relationship between WBS elements. Figure 3-4 represents only one example of the possible decomposition of the elements. It is not intended to be comprehensive or definitive.

3.4 Outputs

3.4.1 Scope Management Plan

The scope management plan is a component of the project or program management plan that describes how the project scope will be defined, developed, monitored, controlled, and verified to the project team and stakeholders. This document is used to control what is in and out of scope. The scope management plan is a component of the overall project management plan.

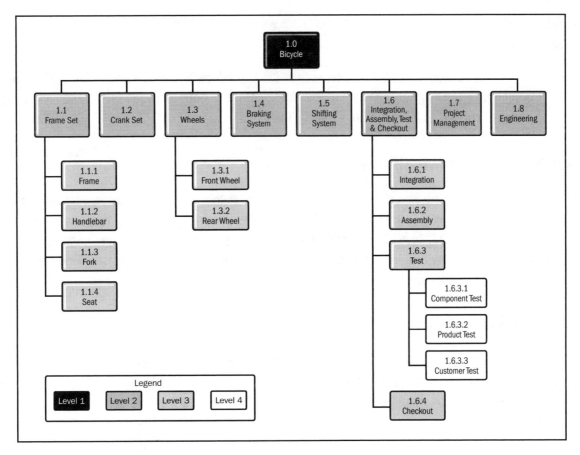

Figure 3-4. Example of WBS for Construction of a Bicycle

3.4.2 Project Scope Statement

The project scope statement helps to enhance an understanding of the scope for the project, whether a product or result is being developed or a service is being delivered. It describes the project scope, major deliverables, assumptions, and constraints, and a description of the work that provides a documented basis for making future decisions, and for confirming or developing a common understanding of the project scope among the stakeholders. With a clear project scope statement, responsible and performing organizations can better plan, organize, and execute the work and deliver the desired product.

3.4.3 Work Breakdown Structure

The work breakdown structure (WBS) is a deliverable-oriented hierarchical decomposition of the work to be executed by the project team to accomplish the project objectives. It organizes and defines the total scope of the project. Each descending level of detail represents an increasingly thorough definition of the project work.

The WBS is extended by establishing control accounts with appropriate work packages associated with each control account.

The WBS translates requirements into elements of work, product, and deliverables. The WBS includes the project management work necessary for communications and meetings required for effective integration management to ensure all deliverables are explicitly identified.

3.4.4 Work Breakdown Structure Dictionary

The work breakdown structure dictionary provides detailed deliverable, activity, and scheduling information about each component in the work breakdown structure. Other information includes: responsible organization, resources required (by skill level), cost estimates, basis of estimates, assumptions, contract information, contract constraints, quality requirements, acceptance criteria and technical references. Figure 3-5 provides an example of a WBS dictionary.

3.4.5 Scope Baseline

The scope baseline is a document or plan officially signed at the sponsor level against which delivery will be compared. It can only be changed with explicit agreement at the original sign-off level or higher. The scope baseline includes the scope statement, the WBS, and the WBS dictionary, and is a component of the project management plan.

WBS Level	WBS Code	Element Name	Definition	Start and End Date	Responsible Organization
1	1.0	Bicycle	All components and subassemblies to design, develop, test, and produce a bicycle.		Project Office
2	1.1	Frame Set	The individual components that together constitute an assembled frame.		Model Shop
3	1.1.1	Frame	The unit tubular steel structure with which other components are attached. Provides basic design and strength.		Metal Engineering
3	1.1.2	Handlebar	Used by the rider to steer the bicycle. Also serves as point of attachment for hand brakes, lights, and other accessories.		Metal Engineering
3	1.1.3	Fork	Attaches wheels to frameset.		Metal Engineering
3	1.1.4	Seat	Padded saddle attached to frame for rider to sit on.		Fabric Engineering
2	1.2	Crank Set	Mechanical linkage for converting rider's pedaling action into rotation of rear wheels to provide propulsion. Part selection is determined by performance specifications and compatibility with other mechanical components.		Model Shop
2	1.3	Wheels	Interface with ground. Specification varies based on materials, weight, and aerodynamic styling.		Model Shop

Figure 3-5. Example of WBS Dictionary for a Bicycle

3.5 Considerations

3.5.1 Constructed with Technical Expertise

Understanding and organizing the project work is the first step in developing a realistic project management plan so that earned value can be deployed as a planning, executing, and monitoring and controlling technique. The WBS is the foundation for all other planning processes, and, as such, it is must be a collaborative effort with participation by all appropriate stakeholders. The WBS enables definition and management of technical requirements and deliverables to meet the project objectives. In addition, the WBS supports technical and project management documentation as well as the change control process.

3.6 Summary

In order to plan, manage, and control a project effectively, there must be a clear description and understanding of the project and product/service scope. The project charter or customer contract, stakeholder needs, and project requirements are the foundations for defining and elaborating the project scope. The scope statement, WBS, and WBS dictionary comprise the scope baseline and will be used by numerous other processes to fully plan the project.

CHAPTER 4

ASSIGN RESPONSIBILITY

4.1 Introduction

Assign responsibility is the process of appointing, designating, and documenting the single person responsible for conducting the execution of the project work. Like most actions in project management, this is an iterative process. The initial organizational structure will be integrated with the WBS. As-needed changes and adjustments are made prior to the achievement of a stable organizational structure. Each element of work has an individual who is responsible and accountable for the scope, schedule, and cost of the work. Inputs and outputs are provided in Figure 4-1.

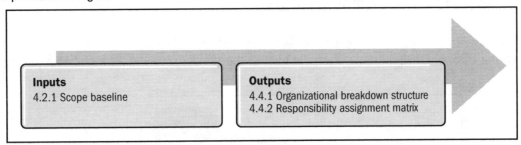

Inputs
4.2.1 Scope baseline

Outputs
4.4.1 Organizational breakdown structure
4.4.2 Responsibility assignment matrix

Figure 4-1. Assign the Responsibility: Inputs and Outputs

4.2 Inputs

4.2.1 Scope Baseline

The scope baseline contains all of the project work against which delivery will be compared.

4.3 Description

4.3.1 Create Organizational Structure

Projects are undertaken within the existing structure of an organization. However, the organizational structure for the project itself needs to be documented to reflect the lines of authority and communication within the project. The project structure can reflect the organization's structure or some other structure depending on the needs of the project and the organization's policies. It must also reflect responsibility for the accomplishment of the work.

4.3.2 Integrate WBS and Organizational Structure

Integrating the WBS on one axis of a matrix, and the organizational structure on the other, shows how the work and the responsibility are matched up. At this stage, the individual who is assigned the responsibility for any given element of work may or may not be identified.

Following the initial work integration, the project manager collaborates with the appropriate organizational managers (frequently called functional or line managers) to identify the individual who is to be assigned responsibility and authority for performing the work to be done. That individual then determines and develops the budget and schedule to accomplish that work (i.e., the what, when, and how much of the work).

4.4 Outputs

4.4.1 Organizational Breakdown Structure

The organizational breakdown structure (OBS) is a hierarchical representation of the project organization that illustrates the relationship between project activities and the responsible organizational units that will perform those activities. It is arranged to relate the control accounts to the organization units.

4.4.2 Responsibility Assignment Matrix

The responsibility assignment matrix (RAM) (see Figure 4-2) shows the integration of the work in the WBS and the OBS, and helps ensure each element of the project scope is assigned to a person or a team.

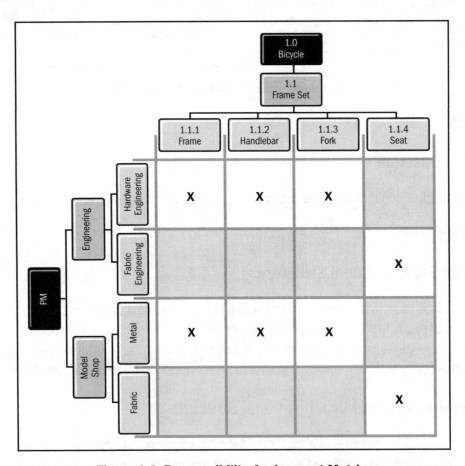

Figure 4-2. Responsibility Assignment Matrix

The RAM delineates levels of control and responsibility and indicates the authority and responsibility levels for the project. The intersection point of the OBS and the WBS is the control account. The individual responsible and accountable for the successful delivery of the scope, schedule, and budget in a control account is the control account manager (CAM).

Each control account can only belong to one WBS element and one OBS element. It is permissible for multiple organizations (frequently called performing organizations) to work on the scope within a control account, but management responsibility and accountability belong to only one organization (the responsible organization).

4.5 Considerations

4.5.1 Level of Detail

While no specific level of detail is appropriate for all projects, the project manager needs to recognize the dangers of keeping that level too high or too low. At too high a level, the size of the control accounts (in budget, schedule, and/or scope) will overwhelm the control account managers (CAMs). At too low a level, the sheer number of control accounts will be, at best, distracting, but more likely detrimental to the successful accomplishment of the work within the parameters of the control account. Additionally, driving the level of the control account down increases the amount of management oversight and intervention required by stakeholders. The level of detail should be managerially consistent with control account manager capability and span of control.

4.5.2 Maintenance

Whenever work and budget moves into, out of, or within the project, one or more control accounts will change. That change should always be reflected on the RAM. Such an approach will give the project manager a continuously updated picture of all of the work and budget that is associated with a project.

4.6 Summary

The WBS is integrated with the project organizational structure to ensure that all work is managed by a responsible and accountable individual. The project organization is documented in a hierarchical format called an organizational breakdown structure (OBS). The OBS is matrixed with the WBS to create a RAM. The intersection of the WBS with the OBS elements determines the control account. The control account manager is responsible and accountable for the scope, schedule, and budget for the work.

CHAPTER 5

DEVELOP SCHEDULE

5.1 Introduction

Develop Schedule is the process of translating all of the WBS elements into a sequential, time-phased model for project execution. Resource loading the schedule model at the activity level is not required for the application of EVM; however, it is a recommended practice that lends credibility to the performance measurement baseline. Inputs and outputs are provided in Figure 5-1.

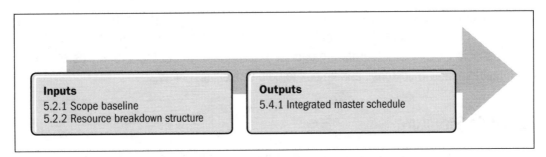

Inputs
5.2.1 Scope baseline
5.2.2 Resource breakdown structure

Outputs
5.4.1 Integrated master schedule

Figure 5-1. Develop Schedule: Inputs and Outputs

The project schedule integrates the activities associated with each WBS element and identifies dependencies between project activities as well as the dependencies that are external to the project. The schedule model can be decomposed and presented at various levels of detail.

This practice standard focuses on those schedule components having specific relevance to the practice of EVM. Therefore it is assumed, for purposes of this chapter, that scheduling processes as outlined in the *PMBOK® Guide* will be followed. For an overview of what is considered good practice on most projects most of the time for scheduling, refer to Chapter 6 on Project Time Management of the *PMBOK® Guide*. For a more extensive treatment on the definition and implementation for project scheduling practices, refer to the *Practice Standard for Scheduling* [5].

5.2 Inputs

5.2.1 Scope Baseline

The scope baseline, comprised of the scope statement, WBS, and WBS dictionary, provides information on all of the product and project deliverables for the project against which delivery will be compared. The scope baseline should include sufficient information to allow project team members to decompose the work into the activities needed to complete the scope of work.

5.2.2 Resource Breakdown Structure

All resources required to complete the activities are identified including people, equipment, materials, supplies, and any other direct or indirect item required to execute the project. In some projects, sites and locations are also resources that may need to be considered for scheduling and cost estimating purposes.

5.3 Description
5.3.1 Schedule Tool

A schedule tool, in combination with a specific scheduling method (such as Critical Path Method), is used to enter the project-specific data including activities, logic sequence, duration estimates, resource estimates (if included), and other useful schedule-related information. The schedule tool processes and dynamically reacts to the project specific data entered into the tool to create a schedule model. The schedule tool selected for any project should include an integrated master schedule that lays out the total scope of the project from start to finish including key milestones and key stakeholder decision points.

5.3.2 Schedule Structure

The schedule model should be structured to reflect the logic of the WBS. The hierarchy may include:

- Higher levels of the WBS

- Control accounts

- Work packages and planning packages

- Activities

All activity relationships should be driven by the logic of the natural relationship between the activities.

5.3.3 Schedule and Budget Relationship

The relationship between the schedule model and the budgeting system is maintained throughout the life of the project. The planned value is derived using the same assumptions as the scheduling model. The same WBS and set of other budget elements (control accounts, work packages, and planning packages) will likely exist in both systems. Certain attributes of these, such as start and finish dates, budgets or "weighting," and organizational responsibility, should always remain consistent between the budget and the schedule.

Once the project schedule model has been reviewed and agreed to by all the project stakeholders, it is saved and stored as the project schedule baseline, which forms the basis for the time-phased peformance measurement baseline. Chapter 10 of this practice standard addresses maintenance of the budget baseline.

The same controls and discipline implemented to manage the budget baseline should be in place for the schedule baseline. For example, just as adjusting the budget baseline because of a cost overrun or underrun condition is discouraged, adjusting the schedule baseline due to an ahead or behind-schedule condition is also not a good practice and is discouraged.

5.4 Outputs

5.4.1 Integrated Master Schedule

The integrated master schedule represents the time phasing for execution of the project's scope of work. The project schedule should reflect the total project scope of work as defined in the WBS. It should be scheduled to a level of granularity and detail needed to plan, implement, and control the project. Both the high-level "master" schedule and the highest level of the WBS represent the overall project scope. Lower levels of the WBS correspond to equivalent levels of the schedule, with this concept extending to control accounts, work packages, and planning packages. Refer to Figure 5-2.

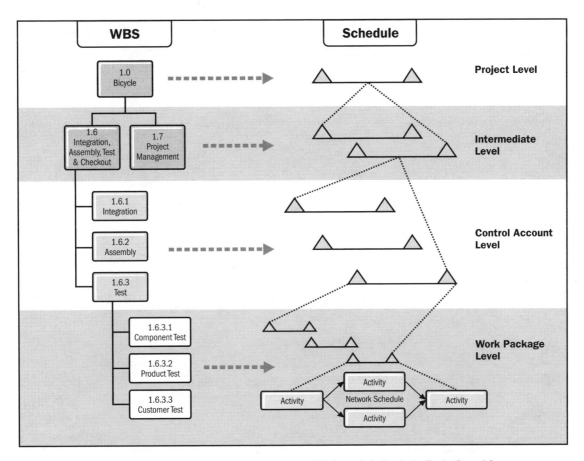

Figure 5-2. Bicycle Project Example—WBS and Schedule Relationships

5.5 Considerations

5.5.1 Schedule Evolution

Project budgeting and scheduling are iterative processes involving the negotiation of project constraints until consensus estimates are achieved among the stakeholders. Therefore the schedule will continue to evolve until such time as the project manager establishes the performance measurement baseline.

5.6 Summary

A properly structured "integrated master schedule" depicts the project team's plan for work accomplishment. It provides the underlying logic for the performance measurement baseline, against which accomplishments will be measured and expected future outcomes will be forecast.

Scheduling from an EVM perspective includes:

- A logic-driven schedule that reflects the scope of work
- Schedule activities aligned to the WBS elements

The project schedule reflects the total project scope of work, as defined in the WBS, and should be scheduled to a level of granularity and detail needed to plan, implement, and control the project.

CHAPTER 6

ESTABLISH BUDGET

6.1 Introduction

Establish Budget is the process of converting external requirements and constraints, such as the project charter, resource availability, cost estimates, and scheduling limitations, into cost budget which supports the planned execution of the project. Inputs and outputs are provided in Figure 6-1.

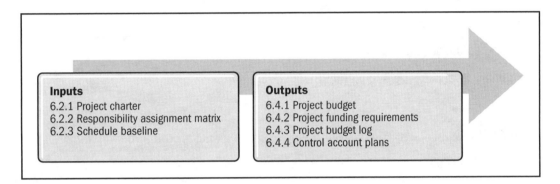

Figure 6-1. Establish Budget: Inputs and Outputs

6.2 Inputs

6.2.1 Project Charter

The project charter provides the high-level project requirements and high-level product or service description of the project.

6.2.2 Responsibility Assignment Matrix

The RAM integrates the work breakdown structure (WBS) and organizational breakdown structure (OBS) identifying control accounts and precisely who is assigned responsibility and accountability for each WBS element. From those key management control points, all earned value data can be summarized.

6.2.3 Schedule Baseline

The schedule baseline is the approved version of a schedule model that is used as a basis for comparison to actual results. The process for establishing a budget baseline is iterative with that of creating the schedule baseline; the two must reconcile and support each other before the performance measurement baseline can be finalized.

6.3 Description

6.3.1 Establish a Budget Structure

Budget elements are tracked throughout the life of the project. The components of the project budget are listed here:

- Project (or contract) budget base (PBB (or CBB))
- Management reserve (MR)
- Performance measurement baseline (PMB)
- Undistributed budget (UB)
- Contingency reserve
- Distributed budget (DB)
- Summary level planning budget (SLPB)
- Control account
- Work package
- Planning package

Refer to Figure 2-4, which illustrates how the budget elements are related.

6.3.2 Develop the Cost Estimate

The cost estimate provides the basis for establishing the budget. Estimates are developed for each work package, planning package, and summary level planning budget. The estimates for work package must be robust enough to support the establishment of the performance measurement baseline, while those for planning packages and summary level planning budgets may have a lower level of detail until enough information is available to support the conversion to work packages. All cost estimates within control accounts must be developed within the time frames established for that work in the schedule baseline. Guidance for developing a cost estimate can be found in the *Practice Standard for Project Estimating* [6].

Once the cost estimates for work packages and planning packages within a control account are completed, they are reviewed by the project manager and the control account manager. The project manager may decide to authorize budget for an amount more, less, or equal to the cost estimate as follows:

- More budget may be authorized if the project manager is aware of likely future events, such as a change in rates, processes, or customer.

- Less budget may be authorized if the project manager is giving the control account manager a stretch goal or holding back reserve.

- Budget equal to the cost estimate may be authorized, particularly if risk analysis and reserves are handled outside of the control account.

6.3.3 Authorize the Work

Authorization is formal permission and direction, to begin a specific project effort, typically a control account. It is a method for sanctioning project work to ensure that the work is done by the identified organization, at the right time, in the proper sequence, and within the allotted budget. In its simplest form, the work authorization process follows these steps:

1. The project manager receives authorization to proceed with the project by means of a project charter or customer contract. This authorization may include limits on the funds available to the project manager and thus the amount of budget that may be authorized.

2. The project manager authorizes the next tier of management to proceed with the assigned work, usually by issuing a work authorization document (WAD). Typically this next level is the control account level, but sometimes there may be one or more additional levels between the total project and the control accounts. If so, each level can receive its own authorization and then continue the authorization within its prescribed, unbroken chain of authorization.

3. Should the organization's system call for it, there may be a step that includes functional manager concurrence or possibly authorization.

4. The control account manager may issue authorization to specific individuals indicating that they should begin work and notifying them of the scope, planned budget (often in hours), and the charge numbers required to be used.

6.3.4 Update the Project Budget Log

As work is authorized for control accounts, entries are made in the project budget log to show the movement of budget from undistributed budget to distributed budget. If the entire project is authorized into control accounts (or control accounts and summary level budgets), then the value of undistributed budget will be zero. Within control accounts, the budget will be authorized to work packages or planning packages. A typical project budget log might be structured in a similar fashion as Figure 6-2.

Budget Log				
Date	**From Account**	**To Account**	**Amount**	**Description**
1/1/2011		UB	$50,000	Initial funding per contract award
1/3/2011	UB	CA001	$25,000	Authorize CA001
1/3/2011	UB	CA002	$20,000	Authorize CA002
1/3/2011	UB	MR	$5,000	Transfer $5K to MR
1/5/2011	CA001	WPA023	$5,000	Authorize WPA023

Figure 6-2. Project Budget Log

6.4 Outputs

6.4.1 Project Budget

The project budget is the authorized time-phased representation of how and when the project budgets will be distributed.

6.4.2 Project Funding Requirements

Total funding requirements and periodic funding requirements are determined based on the project cost estimates. If the funding available and the funding required are not consistent, the project may have to be replanned to meet funding constraints.

6.4.3 Project Budget Log

The project budget log is the central repository for all project budgets. At any time, the project manager should be able to review the project budget log and obtain a complete knowledge of the value and classification for every element of the project budget throughout the life of the project (see Figure 6-2).

6.4.4 Control Account Plans

The detailed plan for a control account is called a control account plan (CAP). The CAP contains all elements and aspects of the control account, some of which include:

- Name of the responsible control account manager

- Description of the work to be done

- Specific milestones to be accomplished

- Work packages that delineate the scope, schedule, and budget (incrementally, cumulative-to-date, and at completion) for specific well-defined tasks within the control account

- Planning packages that delineate the scope, schedule, and budget (incrementally, cumulative-to-date, and at completion) for specific future tasks within the control account

- Estimates to complete, which should be time-phased and may lead to an up-to-date representation of the total expected funding needed (the estimate at completion)

Figure 6-3 shows a sample control account plan.

Control Account				March	April	May	June	Total	Start	Finish
1.6.3	Test	PV	Hours		160	160		320	5-Apr-20XX	28-May-20XX
			Dollars		9600	9600		19200		
		EV	Hours							
			Dollars							
		AC	Hours							
			Dollars							
		ETC	Hours		160	160		320	5-Apr-20XX	28-May-20XX
			Dollars		9600	9600		19200		

Time Now

Work Package				March	April	May	June	Total	Start	Finish
1.6.3.1	Component Test	PV	Hours		160			160	5-Apr-20XX	30-Apr-20XX
			Dollars		9600			9600		
		EV	Hours							
			Dollars							
		AC	Hours							
			Dollars							
		ETC	Hours		160			160	5-Apr-20XX	30-Apr-20XX
			Dollars		9600			9600		
1.6.3.2	Product Test	PV	Hours			80		80	3-May-20XX	14-May-20XX
			Dollars			4800		4800		
		EV	Hours							
			Dollars							
		AC	Hours							
			Dollars							
		ETC	Hours			80		80	3-May-20XX	14-May-20XX
			Dollars			4800		4800		
1.6.3.3	Customer Test	PV	Hours			80		80	17-May-20XX	28-May-20XX
			Dollars			4800		4800		
		EV	Hours							
			Dollars							
		AC	Hours							
			Dollars							
		ETC	Hours			80		80	17-May-20XX	28-May-20XX
			Dollars			4800		4800		

Figure 6-3. Sample Control Account Plan

6.5 Considerations

6.5.1 Budget Versus Funding

One of the key aspects of earned value management is the very specific terminology related to budget and funds. Budget is a work planning element that is earned (i.e., the earned value) when the corresponding work is done. Funds are the amount of money that is available to accomplish the work. One of the benefits of work authorization is that it allows the project manager to manage situations when full funding is not provided.

6.6 Summary

The budgeting process establishes the plan for creating a budget structure, developing the cost estimate, authorizing the work, determining funding requirements, and establishing budget logs and control account plans.

CHAPTER 7

DETERMINE MEASUREMENT METHODS

7.1 Introduction

Determine Measurement Methods is the process used to select the appropriate method of progress evaluation for each work package. During the planning process, the project manager and control account manager determine an approach to the measurement of scope accomplishment for each WBS element assigned to the control account manager. This chapter introduces the principal methods used to determine performance. Inputs and outputs are provided in Figure 7-1.

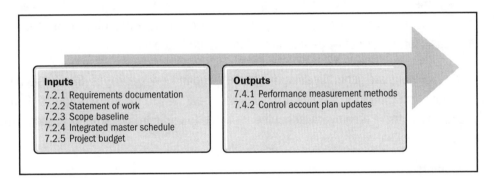

Figure 7-1. Determine Measurement Methods: Inputs and Outputs

7.2 Inputs

7.2.1 Requirements Documentation

Requirements can include contract requirements, business requirements, standards, technical requirements, performance requirements, legal/regulatory requirements, and any other applicable requirements.

7.2.2 Statement of Work

The statement of work is a description of products, results, or services to be delivered by the project.

7.2.3 Scope Baseline

The scope baseline is the approved version of a scope statement, work breakdown structure, and its associated WBS dictionary, that is used for a basis of comparison. The WBS, as part of the scope baseline, identifies all of the deliverables for the project. The WBS dictionary supports the WBS and provides more detailed descriptions of the WBS components. The WBS dictionary will likely include a description of the control accounts and it may include a description of work packages.

7.2.4 Integrated Master Schedule

The integrated master schedule provides the planned dates for performing activities included in the schedule. As a minimum, the project schedule includes a baselined planned start and a finish date for each activity.

7.2.5 Project Budget

The project budget illustrates the time-phased distribution of funds for the planned work. Thus the project budget and the integrated master schedule are key elements to develop the performance measurement baseline (PMB). PMB is established through a process of selecting and applying an appropriate performance measurement method to each work package.

7.3 Description

Earned value is a measure of work performed and a snapshot of work progress at a given point in time. The methods for measuring work performed are selected during project planning prior to commencing the work, and are the basis for performance measurement during project execution.

The earned value methods are generally assigned and applied to work packages. Each work package has its own unique characteristics; therefore, there is not one single best way to measure progress. To accommodate the different types of work, there are several accepted methods to measure work performance. There are three classes of work, as follows:

- Discrete effort
- Apportioned effort
- Level of effort

Each of these classes has one or more measurement methods available, and each method has its own specific characteristics that determine how it is applied to the work.

7.3.1 Discrete Effort

Discrete effort is an activity that can be planned and measured and that yields a specific output. Discrete effort is directly related to specific end products or services with distinct and measurable points, and outputs that result directly from the discrete effort. Four principal measurement methods are available for assignment to work packages classified as discrete effort. The measurement methods used for discrete effort enable accurate measurement of work accomplished. The four discrete effort measurement methods are:

- Fixed formula
- Weighted milestone
- Percent complete
- Physical measurement

Each of these earned value methods has strengths and weaknesses. The specific circumstances and type of project, phase of the project, or type of work package will determine which method is best suited for the measurement method.

.1 Fixed Formula

A fixed formula assigns a specified percentage of the budget value of the work package to the start milestone of the work packages. The remaining budget value percentage is assigned when the work package is completed. The 50/50 method and the 25/75 method are typical and effective methods for detailed, small and short-duration work. A critical point, necessary to ensure correct usage of any fixed-formula method, is that the sum of the milestones in a work package in any given time period must equal the budget value, that is, the PV, in that time period. The choice of a fixed formula should be made based on the nature of the work being accomplished so that the resulting PV and EV is representative of how the work will be executed.

Another important point is to note is that this method is only used on smaller work packages that are planned to start and end within two reporting time periods. The use of fixed formula makes it easy to plan and measure performance but the arbitrary percentage may not accurately represent work performance.

Figure 7-2 shows a work package (1.1.4 Seat) with a budget at completion (BAC) of $4,400. Using the 50/50 fixed-formula method shows earned value (EV) of $2,200 or 50% of the work planned and credited for the measurement period in which the work begins, regardless of how much work has actually been accomplished. The remaining EV of $2,200 or 50% is credited when the work is completed. The start and finish milestone values summarize to the work package BAC of $4,400.

The same example using the 25/75 fixed formula method credits EV of $1,100 or 25% of $4,400 when the work begins and remaining EV of $3,300 or 75% when the work is completed.

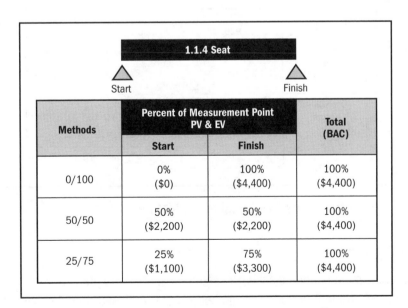

Methods	Percent of Measurement Point PV & EV		Total (BAC)
	Start	**Finish**	
0/100	0% ($0)	100% ($4,400)	100% ($4,400)
50/50	50% ($2,200)	50% ($2,200)	100% ($4,400)
25/75	25% ($1,100)	75% ($3,300)	100% ($4,400)

Figure 7-2. Fixed Formula Methods

Within the fixed-formula method, the 0/100 technique is different from the other techniques. The 0/100 method does not allow any credit to be earned until the work is actually completed. This method is commonly used for receipt of materials and only used on work packages that are planned to start and end within one reporting time period. The CAM and the project manager may agree to any formula to calculate the EV as long as it produces verifiable results that meet the objectives of the project.

.2 Weighted Milestone

A milestone is a significant point or event in the project. The weighted milestone method divides the work package into measurable segments, each ending with an observable milestone; it then assigns a weighted value to the achievement of each milestone. The weighted milestone method is more suitable for longer duration work packages (i.e., those longer than two time periods) that have intermediate and tangible results, or milestones. To be used most effectively, the weighted milestone technique requires at least one interim milestone for each reporting period and does not permit partial credit for incomplete milestones. Figure 7-3 shows a work package (1.4 Braking System) with three milestones (measurement points) that are assigned a specific weighted value. Earned value is accumulated as milestones are completed.

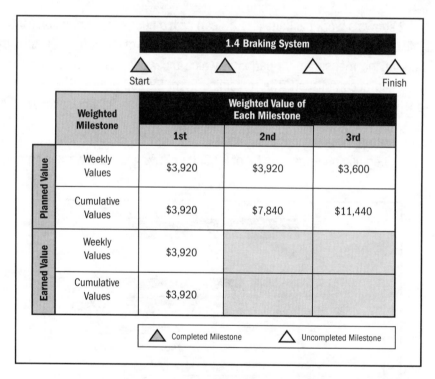

Figure 7-3. Weighted Milestone Method

.3 Percent Complete

The percent complete method shows an estimate of the percentage of work that is complete at the end of each measurement period. This method should be based on objective and quantifiable work completion. The planned value is determined by the time-phased resources required to accomplish the work package. The earned value (EV) is determined by multiplying the work package BAC by the percent complete. Percent complete should be determined in as objective a manner as possible. For example, specifying set criteria, agreed to by relevant stakeholders, for establishing a given percent complete. Figure 7-4 shows a work package (1.3.1 Front Wheel) with a budget of $15,600, when selecting this method. At the end of the second measurement point, 67% of the work (two-thirds of the work) is planned to be completed. Therefore $15,600 multiplied by 67% (2/3) equates to $10,400 for the cumulative PV. In actuality, the organization accomplished 70% of the work at the end of the second measurement point, thus resulting in an earned value of $10,920. It is important to note that work hours expended does not equal deliverables work completed. For example, 50 hours of effort expended on a work package planned for 100 hours does not mean that 50% of the work has been accomplished.

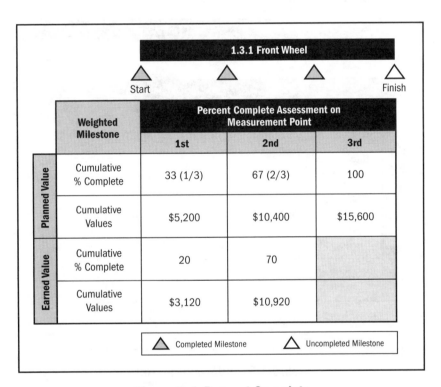

Figure 7-4. Percent Complete

.4 Physical Measurement

The physical measurement, unlike the weighted milestone and the percent complete, can be related more explicitly to the completion of the work. Measurement can include any units that can be explicitly related to the completion of the work. Examples may include the length of cable laid, the area and quantity of concrete poured, and the quantity of spokes in the case of the bicycle's wheel. The method of measurement and specific measurement with the cost or efforts spent should be defined and agreed upon in advance.

7.3.2 Apportioned Effort

Apportioned effort is used for work with a direct, supportive relationship to discrete work. The value for the support task is determined based on the earned value of the referenced base activity. Apportioned effort can include such work as quality assurance, inspection, and testing activities. An apportioned work effort is estimated as a percentage of the referenced discrete work effort. The percent allocation to discrete effort is used when there are sufficient performance records and knowledge of the interrelationship between the apportioned effort and the discrete effort. In Figure 7-5, the discrete effort at the second measurement point is 5,200. The apportioned effort is 10% of the discrete effort. Therefore the apportioned value at the second measurement point is 10% of 5,200 or 520. In actuality, the actual discrete effort accomplished at the end of the second period was 7,800; therefore the apportioned earned value at the second measurement point is 10% of 7,800 or 780.

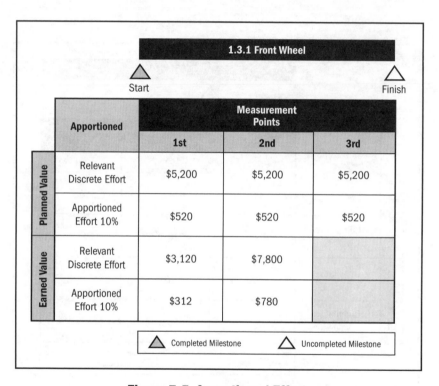

Figure 7-5. Apportioned Effort

7.3.3 Level of Effort (LOE)

Level-of-effort (LOE) activities do not directly produce definitive end products that can be delivered or measured objectively. LOE work, such as project or program management and contract management, consume project resources and should be included in the EVM Planning, Executing, and Monitoring and Controlling Process Groups. LOE effort is not necessarily characterized by a uniform rate of work over a period of time. A planned value is assigned to each LOE task for each measurement period, and this planned value is credited as EV at the end of the measurement period. EV is accrued in line with PV which means LOE activities will not have a schedule variance. However cost variance can be incurred because the actual cost (AC) is usually different from EV. It is also important to note that LOE activities can accrue EV in the absence of AC. See Chapter 9 for more information on SV and CV.

Figure 7-6 shows earned value equal to the planned value at all measurement points.

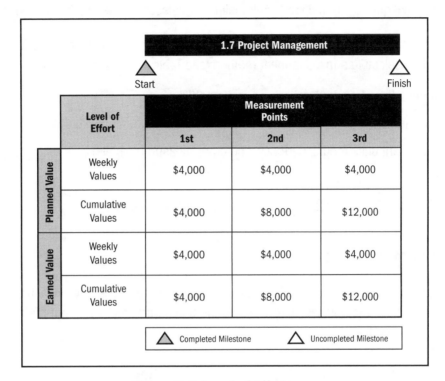

Figure 7-6. Level of Effort

7.4 Outputs

7.4.1 Performance Measurement Methods

The performance measurement method for each work package is selected with careful consideration to the specific characteristics for the type of work. The major drivers to determine the method are duration and the tangibility of the deliverables. Table 7-1 includes guidelines for selecting appropriate measurement methods.

7.4.2 Control Account Plan Updates

Control account plans are established when defining the scope of the project. They are updated with the measurement method information such as:

- Performance measurement method per work package

- Measurement period (e.g., weekly, monthly)

- Measurement unit (e.g., hours, currency, and other measurable unit)

7.5 Considerations

7.5.1 Select the Method

The performance measurement method is selected and determined for each work package based on the duration and physical qualities of the work. A guideline for selecting a method is outlined in Table 7-1.

To select an appropriate method for each unit, several aspects must be considered. Key points for consideration when selecting a measurement method (see Table 7-2) are as follows:

- Characteristics of work (duration and measurability)
- Requirements
- Measurement units (hours, currency, and other measurable units)
- Risk
- Level of accuracy to measure (cost, schedule, and performance)

7.5.2 Rules of Measurement

Organizations may have explicit guidelines or processes for selecting measurement methods. The guidelines should include method selection, measurement accuracy, measurement period, measurement unit, data collection, and reporting.

7.5.3 Measurement of Procurements

The EV for procured materials may be recorded as of the date of receipt, inspection, or installation. When accounting system actual amounts are not available, an estimate of actual costs may be used. The key is to ensure that actual cost is recorded in the same reporting period as the corresponding earned value. The EV for materials should be recorded as close as possible to the point of consumption, but not earlier than receipt.

Table 7-1 Guidelines for Selecting Measurement Method

Type of Work/Tasks		Characteristics	
		Tangible (Measurable)	Intangible (Immeasurable)
Duration	Short (1-2 Periods)	Fixed Formula	Apportioned Effort Level of Effort
	Longer (Exceeds 2 Periods)	Weighted Milestone Percent Complete Physical Measurement	Apportioned Effort Level of Effort

Table 7-2 Key Points on Measurement Methods

Measurement Methods		Key Points to Consider on Determining the Method
Discrete Effort (7.3.1)	Fixed Formula	50/50, 25/75, etc. – Using the 50/50 and 25/75 methods, work is credited for EV as soon as it starts. However, the real progress is invisible and can give a false sense of accomplishment. This measurement method should only be used for work that spans less than two reporting periods.
		0/100 – The 0/100 method does not incrementally credit EV for partial work. Therefore the start of the work is not explicitly reported. This measurement method should only be used for work that is scheduled to start and complete within one reporting period.
	Weighted Milestone	The weighted milestone method has one or more milestones in the measurement period. Each milestone has an objective, verifiable accomplishment that is associated with it. The milestones are weighted to reflect the relative accomplishment of the milestones against the whole.
	Percent Complete	The percent complete method entails an estimate of the percent complete of the BAC at each measurement point. There should be measurable criteria associated with the percent complete measurements, or they can be too subjective and inaccurate.
	Physical Measurement	The evaluation of work progress in the project work packages is related to the physical nature. Whereas testing, measurement procedures, and/or its specifications should be explicit and be agreed upon in advance.
Apportioned Effort (7.3.2)		To use apportioned effort, the project manager must have pragmatic knowledge and validated performance records to create the percent of apportioned effort pertaining to the discrete work package.
Level of Effort (7.3.3)		Level of effort (LOE) can be misused and distort the real progress of project, because PV of the LOE determines EV for each reporting period (there is never a schedule variance) no matter how much of the work is actually performed.

7.6 Summary

The primary goal in choosing a performance measurement method is to have the most objective, accurate, and timely assessment possible of work, schedule, and cost status. There are three classes of work: discrete effort (e.g., measurable work), apportioned effort (e.g., work that is factored to measurable work), and level of effort (e.g., non-measurable work). Within the discrete effort class of work, there are multiple methods for determining earned value. There is only one method for determining earned value within each of the apportioned effort and level of effort classes. Selecting the appropriate method depends on the nature of the work, the duration of the work, and whether or not there are tangible outputs. An incorrect choice of a performance measurement method can result in inaccurate status, and subsequently result in incorrect or ineffective management action.

CHAPTER 8

ESTABLISH PERFORMANCE MEASUREMENT BASELINE

8.1 Introduction

Establish Performance Measurement Baseline is the process of integrating the scope, schedule, and cost baselines into a single project baseline from which to manage and control project performance throughout execution. In addition to the scope, cost, and schedule elements, the performance measurement baseline (PMB) also incorporates undistributed budget (along with its corresponding work) and contingency reserves (alongside with the corresponding risks). The PMB does not include the management reserve. Chapter 6 defines the components of the project budget; the PMB is one aspect of that budget. This chapter discusses how to establish and manage the PMB. Inputs and outputs are shown in Figure 8-1.

The PMB is the basis for project control and, therefore, it should model, as accurately as possible, how the project work and corresponding budget is planned to be executed and earned over time. A poor quality PMB will lead to performance indicators with values that bear no useful relationship to the real status of the project and to the causes of performance variance.

For example, if the work is planned as a gross linear progression over a long period of time, but the physical execution follows an "S-shaped" curve reflecting a varying work rate, the schedule performance metrics are likely to produce a "behind schedule" status in the early stages of the work, even if it is being accomplished at a normal work rate. Likewise, it would produce a false "ahead of schedule" status in the later stages of execution.

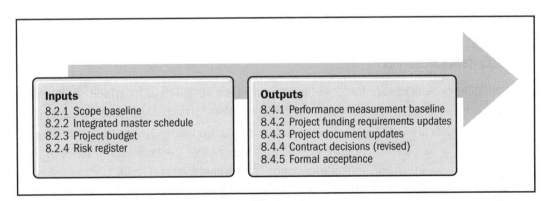

Inputs
8.2.1 Scope baseline
8.2.2 Integrated master schedule
8.2.3 Project budget
8.2.4 Risk register

Outputs
8.4.1 Performance measurement baseline
8.4.2 Project funding requirements updates
8.4.3 Project document updates
8.4.4 Contract decisions (revised)
8.4.5 Formal acceptance

Figure 8-1. Establish Performance Measurement Baseline: Inputs and Outputs

8.2 Inputs

8.2.1 Scope Baseline

The scope baseline includes the project scope statement, the WBS, and the WBS dictionary, against which delivery will be compared.

8.2.2 Integrated Master Schedule

The integrated master schedule establishes the schedule start and finish dates for the project activities to be executed in the project.

8.2.3 Project Budget

The cost performance baseline, as defined in the *PMBOK® Guide*, is the authorized time-phased budget, that is, the planned value (PV). It represents the expected rate at which the project work is to be accomplished. The time-phased budget baseline should not be mistaken for financial information, for example, when invoices are issued or accepted, and payments are authorized and issued. The budget and funding distributions will often differ throughout the life of the project.

8.2.4 Risk Register

The project management plan incorporates risk responses in various forms according to risk response plans. Some responses may require updating the project plan upfront, while others may require changing the plan according to specific emerging circumstances (or risk triggers). For example, a contingency plan may only be implemented when the probability of a high-impact risk increases significantly.

The implementation of risk responses, upfront or later in the project, will affect the expected rate at which the project work will be executed; therefore, the PMB must account for this factor. Information from the risk register, which may end up in the PMB includes the following:

.1 Agreed-Upon Response Strategies

Risk responses for both negative and positive risks can impact the scope, schedule, and cost of the project.

.2 Contingency Reserves

Contingency reserves are for identified risks that are accepted or for which contingent responses are devised. These reserves can fund contingency plans should they need to be implemented or can fund a necessary reaction to a risk after it occurs. Contingency reserves may be global to the overall project or can be allocated by life-cycle phase or other methods. Other types of risk response strategies (i.e., avoid/exploit, mitigate/enhance, and transfer/share) lead to changes to the project management plan and the PMB, and will already be part of the project scope and corresponding budget. Contingency reserves must be incorporated into the PMB.

The use of contingency reserves is a project risk management practice that is not explicitly applied in all existing EVM standards worldwide. Unlike management reserve (MR), which is not in the PMB but is a part of the project budget base (PBB), contingency reserves are considered to be within the PMB. While in commercial environments the explicit use of contingency reserves in the EVM method is quite common, in more traditional- and government-based EVM environments (such as ANSI-748-compliant projects) the only budget within the PMB that is outside of the WBS and is not time-phased is the undistributed budget (UB). In this case, contingency reserve can be treated as a special application of UB with the difference that that it will only be distributed when a risk occurs or a contingency plan is implemented. It is important to note that contingency reserve, while a common practice for EVM as applied in commercial and other international environments, may represent budget within the PMB that is not identified with scope, and thus would not be acceptable within an ANSI-748-compliant environment. Because this practice standard represents a global view of EVM, we will include the application of contingency reserve as an acceptable practice, which it may not be in the user's EVM environment.

It should be noted that, in any case, contingency reserves are not to be used for the purpose of masking overruns. Instead, these reserves are determined as a result of responding to specific identified risks and therefore are to be applied only toward those risks. While it is expected that the contingency reserve will be consumed to accommodate those risks as they occur or as contingency plans are implemented, there can be situations when the risk is greater than initially estimated and extra budget will be needed, requiring a change request. In the opposite case, when there is an overestimation of risk, there will be budget remaining in the contingency reserve at the end of the project, which may not be applied to mask overruns elsewhere in the PMB.

The *Practice Standard for Project Risk Management* [7] provides additional information regarding the use of contingency reserves. For a more detailed discussion on the use of reserves in EVM, refer to Appendix E.

.3 Contract Decisions

Transferring or sharing risk via a contract, as a form of risk response, will lead to the involvement of third parties. This will have an impact on how the project work will be accomplished and how the budget consumption will occur and be monitored. The use of EVM to monitor the performance of subcontracted work requires proper consideration in the PMB. For example, the visibility of work accomplishments and budget consumption will depend on the type of contract and the terms agreed upon with the suppliers.

8.3 Description

8.3.1 Project Management Plan Integration

The project management team analyzes, consolidates, and integrates the information from the scope, schedule, and cost baselines. The information from the risk registers and risk response plans is incorporated into the baseline information, as appropriate.

The granularity of the PMB can be progressively elaborated throughout project execution in an iterative process as the project scope, schedule, and cost estimates are refined into greater detail (see Figure 8-2).

8.3.2 The Project Budget Base (PBB)

The project budget base is defined in Chapter 2. The PBB is established and maintained by project management and it is revised only by appropriately authorized changes and with the concurrence of the customer and other relevant stakeholders as established for the project.

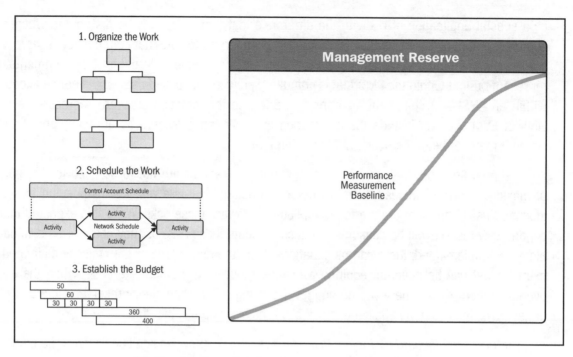

Figure 8-2 Baseline Development Iterative Process

8.3.3 Management Reserve

In most projects, and certainly in major projects, there is considerable uncertainty regarding the magnitude of future events or difficulties, beyond project management team responsibility. To accommodate this uncertainty, a certain amount of the PBB can be identified as management reserve (MR).

The management reserve is part of the PBB, but it is not time-phased and is not part of the performance measurement baseline (PMB). As for contingency reserve, management reserve should not be used to mask performance-related overrun conditions. Rather, it is intended to budget responses to unforeseen risks within the project charter's statement of work.

8.3.4 Performance Measurement Baseline

The performance measurement baseline (PMB) is the budget and schedule against which project performance is measured. It is formed by budgets and is assigned to control accounts, summary level planning budgets, and undistributed budgets. It equals the PBB minus the management reserve. The PMB is maintained by project management, and all changes within the PMB are approved by the project manager.

.1 Undistributed Budget

Undistributed budget (UB) refers to project work that has not yet been incorporated into the WBS during planning (and therefore not yet time-phased). It is a temporary holding account for newly authorized work and budget. In practice, this means that the UB is budget that has not yet been assigned to a control account or to an SLPB. At all times, it must be possible to identify the work that is associated with the UB.

.2 Summary Level Planning Budgets

Desirably, all planned resources, including the resources issued from the undistributed budget to the PMB, should be distributed to control accounts if at all practicable. However, because of the size, criticality, or multiple phases of the project, budgets may be authorized to a higher WBS element level (i.e., above the control account), with corresponding work scope and schedule identified on a project work authorization document—these are the summary level planning budgets (SLPB).

These summary level planning budgets and their corresponding high-level tasks in the WBS (i.e., the summary level planning packages), are assigned to control accounts as soon as sufficient definition of the work is available.

.3 Control Account Budgets

Control account budgets and their corresponding work are assigned and time-phased in accordance with an approved schedule and within control accounts, and may include both direct and indirect costs. Control accounts are time-phased according to the rolling wave concept (see 8.3.5), which requires detailed planning of work packages for as specified number of EV reporting time periods before the scheduled start of the work.

The sum of the budgets in a control account is the budget at completion (BAC) for that control account. The time-phased budget spread of all the resources required to accomplish the control account scope of work is called the planned value (PV). Therefore, the sum of all work package budgets plus the sum of all planning package budgets must equal the control account total budget, in each EV reporting period (typically one month) both incrementally and at completion.

8.3.5 Rolling Wave Planning

Rolling wave planning is an iterative planning technique in which the work to be accomplished in the near term is planned in detail, while the work in the future is planned at a more general level. To accomplish this, a planning window is established during which all planning packages are decomposed into detailed work packages (or summary planning budgets into control accounts). This process continues throughout the project until all planning packages are eventually decomposed into work packages.

8.4 Outputs

8.4.1 Performance Measurement Baseline

The performance measurement baseline (PMB) must include, but is not limited to the following elements:

- Schedule start and completion dates for each work package and planning package in the WBS
- Budget for each work package and planning package, and its time-phased distribution, decomposed by the resources allocated

---

- Time-phased distribution of the quantities of the resources allocated to each work package and planning package

- Description of the risks covered, including: their value, the time period to which they refer and possibly the resource types considered (for example, a cost reserve may include separate limited amounts for external services and for internal resources)

- List of constraints and assumptions regarding work progress, corresponding budget, and resource consumption.

The time-phased information in the PMB should be consistent with the detailed project schedule information at the activity level (for example, the expected time-phased consumption of a specific resource in a work package can be derived from the sequence of its interrelated activities where that resource is allocated).

The information in the PMB must be in sufficient detail to ensure that actual results are properly monitored, recorded, and compared against the planned results. As the project unfolds over time and the project plan is refined into more detail, and as risk reserves are used and converted into work scope and resources, the PMB must be maintained to accurately reflect the expected project outcome as formally approved by the stakeholders.

8.4.2 Project Funding Requirements Updates

The project funding requirements may need to be updated in line with the budgetary decisions made to establish the PMB. This is accomplished in many different ways, and often the funding methodology can be quite different in a government versus a commercial environment.

8.4.3 Project Document Updates

Project documents that may be updated include, but are not limited to the following:

- Scope-related documentation

- Project schedule and time estimates

- Project budget and resource estimates

- Risk register

- Stakeholder register

- Communications management plan

8.4.4 Contract Decisions (Revised)

Establish Performance Measurement Baseline requires agreements with suppliers to ensure that actual progress, cost, and time results are properly monitored for the purpose of the earned value management calculations. For example, assessing the physical progress of subcontracted work requires an adequate level of visibility (how and with what frequency) of the supplier's activities. The supplier must adhere to these requirements and may negotiate extra resources or support from the buyer and this must be reflected in the contract.

8.4.5 Formal Acceptance

There must be only one shared vision of how the project is expected to evolve throughout the life cycle until completion—that is, the performance measurement baseline. A commitment from all stakeholders to this shared vision is a key factor for the success of a project.

8.5 Considerations

8.5.1 Method for Scheduling Level of Effort Work

A project often requires that a certain type of work is executed continuously over a long period of time in a predictable recurring manner, for example, weekly management meetings. Other types of work may also be expected to occur over a reasonably long period of time, but in a less predictable manner, for example, technical support executed "on demand."

This type of ongoing work needs to be planned for in a way that does not distort the earned value performance indicators, and allows for proper monitoring of progress. For less predictable ongoing work, special care must be taken in any attempt to distribute the resources in a nonuniform manner, which often requires further decomposition of the scope.

Regardless of the method used to deal with this type of work, proper consideration of the impact on the performance indicators is required and the underlying assumptions must be clear when interpreting them. The effort required and the feasibility of monitoring actual results and replanning the project must also be taken into consideration.

8.5.2 Method for Allocating Indirect Costs

Organizational indirect costs (sometimes referred to as "overheads") are often aimed at supporting the execution of various projects within a portfolio or program, especially in project-oriented organizations. In this type of environment, allocating the correct amount of indirect costs to a project is important for the purpose of controlling the organization's efficiency, profitability, and competitiveness. For example, an underestimated amount of indirect costs may lead to a project that appears to generate a profit to the organization, whereas a loss is being incurred. Likewise, an overestimated overhead may lead to prices that are not competitive, thereby leading to a loss of feasible business opportunities. Reducing the amount of unallocated indirect costs to a residual level in a project-based business model is essential for the effective management of each project and of the organization's overall business.

Indirect costs should be properly allocated and budgeted as appropriate within the PMB. These indirect budgets may be held separately or allocated within each control account, per organizational policies. Thus the entire budget for the project should be a summation of both direct and allocable indirect costs. The responsibility for budgeting and managing indirect costs should be assigned explicitly to an individual or organizational group.

8.5.3 Impact of Different Types of Resources and Costs

When the PMB is established, it is important to take into consideration the measurement methods selected (see Chapter 7), as these will affect when EV performance is taken. The time phasing of PV in turn will be reflected in the PMB. Comparison between the EV and PV will determine the schedule performance and any misalignment may impact this metric.

8.5.4 Method for Incorporating Contingency Reserves into the PMB

When developing the PMB, the amount of contingency reserves needed (see 8.2.4.2), and where it will be held, must be determined. There are various methods and alternatives specific to organizations and project types. Many applications of EVM using software tools in an ANSI 748 environment may not have the capability to establish and maintain visibility of contingency reserve. However, as discussed earlier, contingency reserve is a common management tool in many environments. Contingency reserve is a reserve based on a risk analysis of the baseline (see Appendix E, Integration of Risk Management and EVM). In some environments, contingency reserve is considered a "funding reserve" owned by the customer for allowance of a project's cost growth in a cost plus contracting environment. However, in this practice standard, contingency reserve is a reserve within the PMB managed by the project manager for the incorporation of realized risks. The value of contingency reserve may be established by identification of discrete risks within the PMB or may be based on a statistical risk assessment. Regardless, the contingency reserve allows for adjusting the PMB, that is, it provides additional flexibility due to the realization of project risks. Like management reserve, it is permissible for there to be remaining contingency reserve at project completion. In this case, it is unused, removed from the PMB, and the budget at completion is set to the cumulative EV (PV). When the decision is made by the project manager to utilize contingency reserve during the project's execution, it is added to future baseline periods in response to realized risks. It is not permissible to adjust past baselines, as this could be viewed as the revision of a baseline for the intent of masking variances. The establishment of contingency reserve should be made under the cognizance of the project manager, and, subsequently, the application of contingency reserve to control accounts should follow a disciplined process under the control of the project manager (much like the application of management reserve).

8.5.6 Integration of Subcontractor Baselines

As referred to in 8.4.4, proper contractual agreements with suppliers are essential to ensure that subcontracted work is reflected appropriately in the PMB. The PMB must be aligned with the way in which information will be used to monitor progress and measure actual costs for the subcontracted work. The supplier's level of maturity, culture, and expertise in using earned value management will impact the contract. The contractual requirements for earned value must be feasible, discourage resistance, encourage suppliers to provide accurate information about progress, and stimulate the supplier's performance. The suppliers may or may not use EVM to control the internal performance of their work, but they must provide the necessary information for EVM to be implemented at the project level (i.e., with regard to the buyer's perspective).

8.6 Bicycle Project Example

In our bicycle example (see Figure 8-3), the total project scope in the WBS has a budget of $277,040. This is the distributed budget and no undistributed budget is being considered. The spread of this budget over the planned schedule forms the planned value (PV) in the earned value method.

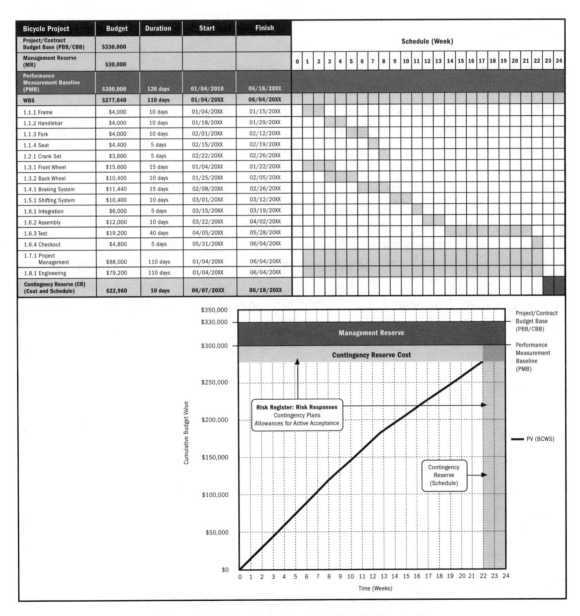

Figure 8-3. Baselines for the Bicycle Example

Based on risks that are under the control of the project management team, and which were identified, analyzed, and responded to, a contingency reserve of $22,960 (cost) and of 10 days (time) was planned to fund contingency plans and reactions to accepted risks as necessary. The project budget plus the contingency reserve form the performance measurement baseline (PMB) against which the project performance will be measured. The PMB for building the bicycle therefore totals $300,000, spread over a period of time of 220 days.

A management reserve of $30,000, representing 10% of the PMB, was constituted by management to account for risks for which the project management team is not accountable (sometimes referred to as "unknown unknowns"). The management reserve plus the PMB forms the project budget base (PBB), also called the contract budget base (CBB) when the project is run under a contract.

8.7 Summary

Establishing the performance measurement baseline (PMB) provides the reference against which performance is measured. The PMB must be an accurate model of how the project is expected to be implemented over time, integrating scope, cost, time, and risk-planning elements. It provides an agreed-upon basis for the purpose of performance measurement for project monitoring and controlling. Once the PMB is approved, performance measurement can begin.

The process of establishing the PMB must take into account some important considerations to ensure that it can effectively incorporate future project changes, the progressive detailing of the project plan (rolling wave), and the way in which risk is being managed. Level-of-effort activities, indirect costs, and different types of resources must be properly considered and incorporated into the PMB. Resource consumption must be properly accounted for to ensure the correct calculation of the project actual cost so it is comparable to the project earned value. The PMB must also incorporate subcontracted work, requiring adequate contractual agreements with suppliers with regard to the collection and use of earned value management information, as appropriate.

CHAPTER 9

ANALYZE PROJECT PERFORMANCE

9.1 Introduction

Analyze Project Performance is the process of comparing actual project cost and schedule performance to the performance measurement baseline for the purposes of analyzing the current status of a project. The primary purpose of EVM is to provide management with a rigorous and complete understanding of the project's cost and schedule performance, and a rational forecast of an anticipated end state for each. This understanding is essential for making good decisions while analyzing the project, exploring opportunities, and mitigating undesired variances. Another purpose of EVM data is to allow for early indication of expected final costs and schedule completion. This analysis provides a prediction of future project performance.

By deploying an EVM system on the project, various metrics can be produced that address the project's cost and schedule for past, current, and future conditions. These metrics may be represented in many data forms and graphics and provide an effective means to communicate a common understanding of the project to all stakeholders. (See Figure 9-1 for the inputs and outputs for this process.)

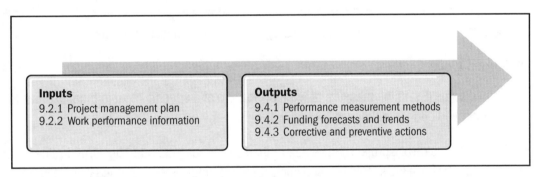

Inputs
9.2.1 Project management plan
9.2.2 Work performance information

Outputs
9.4.1 Performance measurement methods
9.4.2 Funding forecasts and trends
9.4.3 Corrective and preventive actions

Figure 9-1. Analyze Project Performance: Inputs and Outputs

9.2 Inputs

9.2.1 Project Management Plan

The following components in the project management plan are used to analyze project performance:

- **Performance measurement baseline (PMB).** The performance measurement baseline is used to compare planned performance with actual performance to determine project status.

- **Variance thresholds**. This indicates the acceptable range of variances.

- **Subsidiary management plans.** The cost management plan, schedule management plan, scope management plan, and any other management plans that are used to provide guidance in managing and controlling the project.

9.2.2 Work Performance Information

Work performance information includes information about project progress, such as which deliverables have started, what the progress of the deliverables is, and which deliverables have finished. This information is used to determine earned value. It also includes information on costs that have been authorized and incurred. This information is used to determine actual cost.

Earned value management (EVM) relies on four key data points:

- Planned value
- Earned value
- Actual cost
- Budget at completion

The planned value is represented in the performance measurement baseline, as is the budget at completion. The earned value and actual costs are updated as the project progresses. While it is most common to use monetary units to calculate and report earned value, it is possible to convert these to other units such as labor hours for work to be issued and progressed.

.1 Planned Value

Planned value (PV) is the authorized, time-phased budget assigned to accomplish the scheduled work. At any given point on a time line, PV describes how much of the project work was planned to be performed.

.2 Earned Value

Earned value (EV) is the measure of work performed at a specific point in time, expressed in terms of the approved budget authorized for that work.

The earned value of a project can be determined by various methods. The earned value methodology used to plan the baseline should be used consistently to determine the earned value. Figure 9-2 shows the earned value at "time now," and indicates that less work than planned has been accomplished.

.3 Actual Cost

Actual cost (AC) is the realized cost incurred for the work performed during a specific time period. In order for EVM analysis to be reliable, AC must be recorded in the same time period as EV and for the same activity or work breakdown structure component as EV. For example, recording AC for accomplished work several months after EV has been recorded for the same work could significantly distort the EVM data. Figure 9-2 shows the actual cost at time now, and indicates that the organization has spent more than it planned to spend in order to achieve the work performed to date.

.4 Budget At Completion

Budget at completion (BAC) is the sum of all the budgets established for the work to be performed.

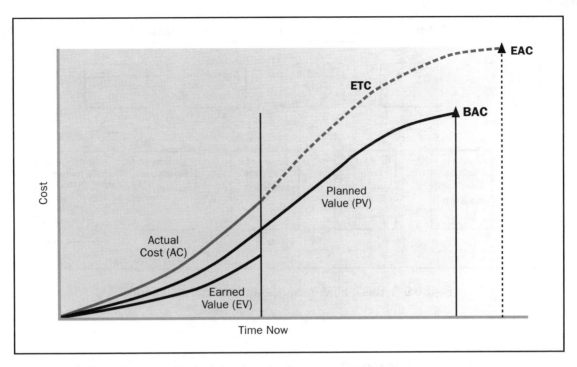

Figure 9-2. Graphic View of the EVM Data

9.3 Description

9.3.1 Performance Analysis

Earned value analyzes project performance by calculating performance variances and performance indices. Common variances include:

- Schedule variance (SV)
- Cost variance (CV)

Common indices include:

- Schedule performance index (SPI)
- Cost performance index (CPI)
- To complete performance index (TCPI)

These variances and indices are summarized in Figure 9-3.

To demonstrate how the various calculations are applied, the following project assumptions will be used as an example to assess work performance (assume data is reported in dollars):

PV = 40 (represents the work planned up to time now)

EV = 32 (represents the work performed up to time now)

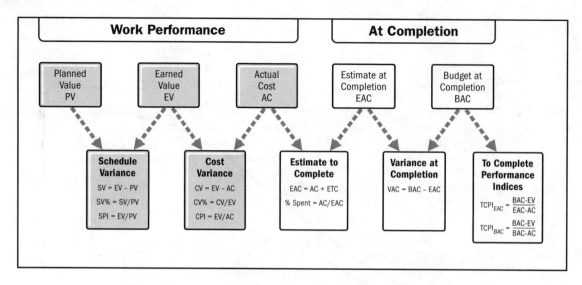

Figure 9-3. Basic EVM Variance and Index Calculations

AC = 48 (represents the cost incurred for the work performed up to time now)

BAC = 150 (represents the total authorized budget)

.1 Schedule Analysis

Schedule variance is very often misinterpreted as a time-based indicator, for example, are we early or late and by how much? It is not a time-based indicator, but rather an indication of the physical status (how much of the work has been accomplished).

The schedule variance (SV) determines whether a project is ahead of or behind schedule in accomplishing work. It is calculated by subtracting the planned value (PV) from the earned value (EV). A positive value indicates more work has been accomplished than planned; a negative value indicates that less work has been accomplished than planned. For our example:

$$SV = EV - PV$$

$$-8 = 32 - 40$$

The schedule variance can be expressed as a percentage by dividing the schedule variance (SV) by the planned value (PV):

$$SV\% = SV/PV$$

$$-20\% = -8/40$$

This means that 20% of the work planned to have been completed has not been accomplished.

The schedule performance index (SPI) indicates how the project team is working compared with the plan. SPI is calculated by dividing the earned value (EV) by the planned value (PV). For our example:

$$SPI = EV/PV$$

$$0.80 = 32/40$$

This schedule performance index indicates that work is being accomplished at 80% of the planned rate. A value of less than 1.0 indicates less work is being accomplished than was planned. Additional emerging techniques for time-based schedule analysis using EVM data are described in Appendix D.

.2 Cost Analysis

The cost variance (CV) shows whether a project is in an over-budget or under-budget condition. This measure is determined by subtracting the actual cost (AC) from the earned value (EV). The CV for our example shows:

$$CV = EV - AC$$

$$-16 = 32 - 48$$

The CV can be expressed as a percentage by dividing the cost variance (CV) by the earned value (EV).

$$CV\% = CV/EV$$

$$-50\% = -16/32$$

In other words, to date, the project is 50% over budget for the work performed.

Earned value and actual cost can also be used to calculate the cost performance index (CPI), which is one of the clearest indicators of the cost efficiency of a project. CPI gages how cost efficient the team is in using its resources. It is determined by dividing the earned value (EV) by the actual cost (AC). With regard to our example, the CPI is:

$$CPI = EV/AC$$

$$0.67 = 32/48$$

This means that for every $100 expended, $67 of the budgeted value is earned. A value of less than 1.0 indicates that more money is being spent than planned to accomplish the budgeted work and is an overrun condition.

Figure 9-4 shows what the EVM performance measures indicate about a project with regard to its planned work schedule and resource budget.

Performance Measures		Schedule		
		SV > 0 & SPI > 1.0	SV = 0 & SPI = 1.0	SV < 0 & SPI < 1.0
Cost	CV > 0 & CPI > 1.0	Ahead of schedule under budget	On schedule under budget	Behind schedule under budget
	CV = 0 & CPI = 1.0	Ahead of schedule on budget	On schedule on budget	Behind schedule on budget
	CV < 0 & CPI < 1.0	Ahead of schedule over budget	On schedule over budget	Behind schedule over budget

Figure 9-4. Interpretations of Basic EVM Performance Measures

9.3.2 Forecasting

As the project progresses, forecasts can be developed for cost and schedule performance. Common forecasting data includes:

- Estimate to complete
- Estimate at completion
- Variance at completion
- To-complete performance index
- These forecasts are summarized in Figure 9-3.

.1 Estimate to Complete

The estimate to complete (ETC) is the expected cost needed to complete all of the remaining work for a control account, work package, or the project. There are two ways to develop the estimate to complete (ETC). The most accurate method is to develop a new, detailed, bottom-up estimate based on an analysis of the remaining work. This is sometimes referred to as a management ETC. As a check on these management estimates, organizations can use a *calculated* or *statistical* ETC, based on the efficiency-to-date measured by the CPI (and sometimes the SPI). A common equation for the statistical ETC is:

$$ETC = (BAC - EV)/CPI$$

Using the sample provided above yields the following:

$$177 = (150 - 32)/0.667$$

.2 Estimate at Completion

Estimate at completion (EAC), is the expected total cost of a control account, work package, or the project when the defined scope of work will be completed. The formal EAC for a project should be estimated by the project team; however EACs may also be calculated based on performance to date. The EAC is typically based on the actual cost incurred for work completed (AC), plus an estimate to complete (ETC) for the remaining work. There are two distinct methods for deriving an EAC value: analytical and statistical.

The analytical approach is a manual, bottom-up summation by the project manager and the project team utilizing their expectation of future conditions and challenges to assess an accurate forecast of project costs.

The management ETC can be added to the actual cost (AC) to derive the management estimate at completion (EAC). For this calculation, assume a management ETC of 142.

EAC = AC + ETC

190 = 48 + 142

The statistical approach utilizes EVM data to project an EAC and is often called an independent EAC (IEAC) because it is independent of any future project or environmental conditions. It is merely a projection of the future project outcome based on past data. The IEAC is independent of human intervention, such as corrective action and risk responses. The use of Independent EAC calculations is a good validation of the project EAC; however it should not be substituted as the formal EAC for the project.

The statistical ETC can be used to determine the calculated estimate at completion (EAC), which the team can compare with the management or formal EAC. For our project, the ETC and EAC can be independently calculated as follows:

225 = 48 + 177

Note that this EAC formula is equivalent to the following:

EAC = BAC/CPI

225 = 150/0.667

The obvious conclusion is that if the project continues at the same cost efficiency (CPI) for the remainder of the project (a likely occurrence), the total hours spent will be 225, rather than the 190 that is forecast.

Table 9-1 is a summary of some of the independent EAC calculations that can be performed and the assumptions associated with each.

.3 Variance at Completion

The cost variance at completion (VAC), derived by subtracting the EAC from the BAC, forecasts the amount of budget deficit or surplus at the end of the project. The VAC shows the team whether the project is forecasted to finish under or over budget.

VAC = BAC − EAC

−40 = 150 − 190

Table 9-1. Independent EAC Assumptions and Calculations

Assumption	Example Formula
Future cost performance will be performed at the budgeted rate	EAC = AC + (BAC−EV) Data Example: EAC = 48 + (150 − 32) = 166
Future cost performance will be the same as all past cost performance	EAC = AC + [(BAC−EV)/CPI] = BAC / CPI Data Example: EAC = 48 + [(150 − 32)/0.67] = 150/0.67 = 225
Future cost performance will be the same as the last three measurement periods (i, j, k)	EAC = AC + [(BAC − EV) / ((EV$_i$ + EV$_j$ + EV$_k$) / (AC$_i$ + AC$_j$ + AC$_k$)]
Future cost performance will be influenced additionally by past schedule performance	EAC = AC + [(BAC − EV) / (CPI x SPI)] Data Example: EAC = 48 + [(150 − 32) / (0.67 x 0.80)] = 269.3
Future cost performance will be influenced jointly in some proportion by both schedule and cost indices	EAC = AC + [(BAC − EV) / (0.8 CPI + 0.2 SPI)] Data Example: EAC = 48 + [(150 − 32) / (0.8 x 0.67) + (0.2 x 0.80)] = 218.2

In other words, the project team is forecasting that the project will cost an additional 40 dollars worth of resources than originally planned. This can be expressed as a percentage by dividing VAC by BAC.

$$VAC\% = VAC/BAC = -26.7\% = -40/150$$

.4 To-Complete Performance Index

The TCPI is a comparative measure. It compares work completed to date with budget required to complete the remaining work. The performance efficiency needed to complete the project is often more, sometimes much more than any previous level of performance achieved. The TCPI data can be used as the basis for a discussion which explores whether the performance required is realistically achievable.

The to-complete performance index (TCPI) is the calculated projection of cost efficiency that must be achieved on the remaining work to meet a specified management goal, such as the BAC or EAC. It is the ratio of remaining work to the remaining budget.

Since EAC is clearly a reflection of the expected final cost of the effort, the intent of using the EAC in the formula is clear, that is, EAC − AC equals the remaining budget. The TCPI for achieving the EAC is calculated by dividing the budget for the remaining work by the estimate to complete:

$$TCPI_{EAC} = (BAC - EV)/(EAC - AC)$$

$$0.83 = (150 - 32)/(190 - 48)$$

This means that in order for the project to achieve the EAC, performance must improve from the existing CPI of 0.67 to a TCPI of 0.83 for the remaining work.

The TCPI for achieving the BAC is calculated by dividing the budget for the remaining work by the total budget less cumulative AC:

$$TCPI_{BAC} = (BAC - EV)/(BAC - AC)$$
$$1.16 = (150 - 32)/(150 - 48)$$

This means that in order for the project to achieve the BAC, performance needs to improve from an already experienced CPI of 0.67 to a TCPI of 1.16 for the performance of the remaining work—not a likely occurrence.

The TCPI is most useful when compared with the CPI. If the TCPI is greater than the CPI, then the specified endpoint (EAC or BAC) may be understated. Increasing the EAC will cause the TCPI to decrease, thereby denoting that the projected cost efficiency will be more in line with the current CPI. Note that since an increase to the BAC requires a commensurate increase in the scope of work, it is not possible to project cost efficiency more in line with the CPI by increasing the BAC. If the TCPI is less than the CPI, then the specified endpoint may be overstated.

If the EAC is used in the denominator of the TCPI, the resulting number shows how efficient the project needs to be in order to achieve the EAC.

If the BAC is used in the denominator of the TCPI, the resulting number shows how efficient the project needs to be in order to achieve the BAC.

These variances, indices, and forecasts can be used to answer key project management questions as listed in Table 9-2.

Table 9-2. EVM as it Relates to Project Management Situations

Project Management Question	EVM Performance Measures
How are we doing timewise?	Schedule Analysis & Forecasting
- Are we ahead or behind schedule?	- Schedule Variance (SV)
- How efficiently are we using time?	- Schedule Performance Index (SPI)
How are we doing cost-wise?	Cost Analysis & Forecasting
- Are we under or over our budget?	- Cost Variance (CV)
- How efficiently are we using our resources?	- Cost Performance Index (CPI)
- How efficiently must we use our remaining resources?	- To-Complete Performance Index (TCPI)
- What is the project likely to cost?	- Estimate at Completion (EAC)
- Will we be under or over budget?	- Variance at Completion (VAC)
- What will the remaining work cost?	- Estimate to Complete (ETC)

9.3.3 Percentage Comparisons

Comparing the percent complete to the percent spent is another way of analyzing the project status. The percent complete is the percent of scope accomplished as compared to the total scope of the project.

$$\%\text{Complete} = EV/BAC$$

$$21.3\% = 32/150$$

The percent complete is compared to the percent spent, which is the amount of actual costs compared to the total forecast of costs on a project, that is, the EAC.

$$\% \text{ Spent}_{EAC} = AC/EAC$$

$$25.3\% = 48/190$$

However, similar to the TCPI calculation and the acceptance of all of the limitations therein, it is sometimes useful to compare the actual costs to the total budget for the project.

$$\% \text{ spent}_{BAC} = AC/BAC$$

$$32\% = 48/150$$

9.3.4 Trend Analysis

Identifying trends in the performance metrics can help a project manager decipher or anticipate a potential performance problem. For instance, a cumulative cost performance index (CPI) that is within an acceptable range, but has been trending down toward a pre-established threshold for that index for several measurement periods, may be cause for some concern and prompt an examination of the underlying cause of the trend. If the trend is seen at the project level, the WBS will enable the manager to "drill down" to lower levels to see what underlies the trend.

9.4 Outputs

9.4.1 Performance Measurement Methods

Performance measurements include the calculated CV, SV, CPI, and SPI values for the various WBS to control accounts. Based on the data of the project, the summary shown in Table 9-3 can be made.

Table 9-3. Summary of Performance Measurements for WBS Components

Schedule		Cost	
SV	−8	CV	−16
SV%	−20%	CV%	−50%
SPI	0.800	CPI	0.67

According to the project schedule, $40 of work were completed at this point in time; however only $32 of work has been accomplished. This means the project is $8, or 20%, behind schedule with an SPI of 0.800. The $32 of work accomplished, however, has taken 48 to complete, giving the project a $16 negative cost performance, a cumulative overrun of 50%, and a CPI of 0.667.

9.4.2 Funding Forecasts and Trends

Funding forecasts can include a management EAC and a comparison of a range of calculated EACs (see Table 9-4).

Table 9-4. Funding Forecast Examples

EAC	
Management	190.0
Math	166.0
CPI only	225.0
CPI x SPI	269.3
0.8 CPI+0.2 SPI	218.2
VAC	
VAC	−40.0
VAC%	−26.7%
TCPI	
$TCPI_{EAC}$	0.83
$TCPI_{BAC}$	1.16

For the authorized scope of this effort, there is a total budget of $150; however, the project team is forecasting an EAC of $190 for that scope of work. Based on the management EAC, a projected overrun at completion of $40 is expected.

Using knowledge of the past challenges and future conditions, the team developed a management EAC of $190. If the existing variance is the only variance, and the rest of the work comes in on budget, the EAC will be 166. However, if the team continues to perform at the same cost efficiency for the remainder of the project, it will take them a total of $225 to complete. Since the project is behind schedule, the project could take from $218.2 to $269.3 to complete. The management team should be under increasing pressure to revise to a higher number the management EAC, or develop some plausible ways to reduce expected future costs.

The project, in total, is 21.3% complete, and has spent 25.3% of the projected forecast of costs (see Figure 9-5).

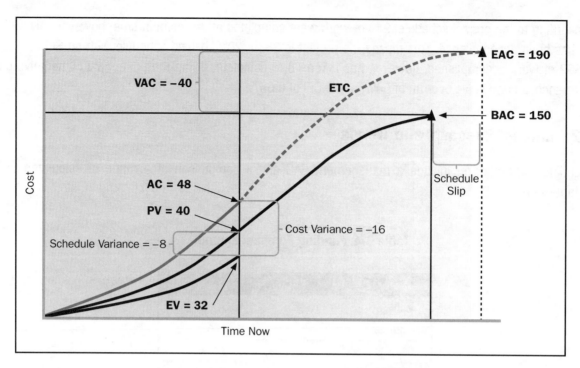

Figure 9-5. Graphic Summary of Project Status

9.4.3 Corrective and Preventive Actions

Based on the analysis of project performance and trends, it may be appropriate to conduct a root cause analysis and recommend preventive actions to keep the project from crossing a performance threshold, or recommend corrective actions to bring performance back in line with expected performance.

9.5 Considerations

9.5.1 Management by Exception

EVM provides an organization with the capability of practicing "management-by-exception" on its projects. This practice contributes greatly to the efficiency and effectiveness of project management, by allowing managers and others to focus on project execution and invoke control actions only when and where they are needed. EVM performance measures, used in conjunction with the project work breakdown structure (WBS), provide the objective data needed to practice "management-by-exception."

Using EVM, an organization can establish acceptable levels of performance for a project and its work tasks. Variance percentages and efficiency indices are most often used. For instance, an organization may consider a cost variance (CV) of plus or minus 10% from the EV to be an acceptable range of variance. For example, some organizations color code their performance thresholds. This in no way suggests that an increasing variance should not and could not be dealt with until it crosses the threshold. The thresholds generally define formal reporting parameters. While a negative variance is potentially problematic, a positive variance may represent an opportunity.

Because EVM is usually measured at the control account level, where the scope, schedule, and cost of work are planned and controlled, "management-by-exception" also starts at this level. EVM performance measures are used to determine whether variance thresholds have been exceeded.

9.5.2 Communication with Earned Value Data

The project team is frequently held accountable for explaining the status of the project using earned value data, and making forecasts as to the probable project outcomes. Often this entails explaining the cost, schedule, and at-completion variances. When communicating variances, it is important that the team describes the cause, impact, and any corrective actions associated with these variances. Responsibility for managing the corrective actions should be assigned to the responsible manager, and the status of corrective actions identified in the past should be addressed.

Earned value management can provide a great deal of useful information to key stakeholders about a project. However, the level and type of information needed about a project may vary greatly from one stakeholder to another. The client, owner, or upper management may simply need a top-line report that indicates whether a project is on time and within budget. By contrast, the project manager will need much more detail in order to make any necessary adjustments to the project. Graphs of variance and efficiency data are helpful tools in communicating earned value analytics. Computer software, especially when developed specifically for project management and EVM, is capable of producing such graphs.

A number of different methods have evolved for presenting EVM data. These methods are designed to address diverse stakeholder needs. Several of these methods may be used on a given project to meet the needs of different stakeholder audiences. This short list of presentation methods is not, by any means, all encompassing. Other methods such as pie charts, dials, scatter grams, and radar or bulls-eye charts, have all been used and can be very effective methods of conveying EVM information. The most commonly used methods include:

- Tables
- Bar charts
- S-curves

.1 Tables

A tabular format can be an effective method for displaying the EVM results by project component. The individual components, for example, WBS elements, of a project could be listed down one side with various EVM calculations going across. A table format provides the project manager and other top-level stakeholders with a complete, concise picture of what is happening with each major component of the project. It can be used as a logical follow-up to an S-curve to provide more detail on where the project is at a given point in time.

.2 Bar Charts

Bar charts can be a useful tool for comparing data such as PV to EV, or AC to EV, etc.

.3 Curves

S-curves, like the ones used earlier in this section, illustrate the cumulative performance metrics of EVM. The typical S-curve is displayed on an X–Y axis with time shown on the X axis and resources shown on the Y axis. This type of display can be very effective for providing a quick look at the overall performance of an activity, a control account, or a project.

9.6 The Bicycle Case Study

A properly designed earned value management system will generate a great deal of data and metrics that are timely, reliable, and useful to management. The purpose is to provide all project stakeholders, both those working on the project team and those outside the project, with information that can be used to monitor the project status, understand the causes of variation, make decisions, and communicate project performance to others. This information not only includes current project conditions and past performance, but it also includes forecasts concerning the project's future performance.

9.6.1 Analyzing the Data

Figures 9-6 and 9-7 are tabular presentations of the bicycle project's data. Figure 9-6 represents the project's earned value data as of the end of Period 6.

Bicycle Project Data	PV	EV	AC	CPI	SPI	TCPI	% Complete	BAC	EAC
Project Budget Baseline Management Reserves								330,000 30,000	287,110 –
Performance Measurement Baseline Undistributed: Contingency Reserves	87,570	74,576	64,150	1.16	0.85	1.01	24.9	300,000 22,960	287,110 22,960
Sum of WBS Elements	87,520	74,576	64,150	1.16	0.86	1.01		277,040	264,150
1.1.1 Frame	4,000	4,000	4,500	0.89	1.00	0.00	100.0	4,000	4,500
1.1.2 Handlebar	4,000	4,000	3,500	1.14	1.00	0.00	100.0	4,000	3,500
1.1.3 Fork	4,000	2,000	2,000	1.00	0.50	1.00	50.0	4,000	4,000
1.1.4 Seat	–	–	–	–	–	–	0.0	4,400	4,400
1.2.1 Crank Set	–	–	–	–	–	–	0.0	3,600	3,600
1.3.1 Front Wheel	15,600	15,600	5,000	3.12	1.00	0.00	100.0	15,600	5,000
1.3.2 Back Wheel	10,400	10,400	9,750	1.07	1.00	0.00	100.0	10,400	9,750
1.4.1 Braking System	3,920	1,176	2,000	0.59	0.30	1.03	10.3	11,440	12,000
1.5.1 Shifting System	–	–	–	–	–	–	0.0	10,400	10,400
1.6.1 Integration	–	–	–	–	–	–	0.0	6,000	6,000
1.6.2 Assembly	–	–	–	–	–	–	0.0	12,000	12,000
1.6.3 Test	–	–	–	–	–	–	0.0	19,200	19,200
1.6.4 Checkout	–	–	–	–	–	–	0.0	4,800	4,800
1.7.1 Project Management	24,000	17,600	17,600	1.00	0.73	0.97	20.0	88,000	90,000
1.8.1 Engineering	21,600	19,800	19,800	1.00	0.92	1.08	25.0	79,200	75,000

Figure 9-6. Bicycle Data by WBS as of Period 6

	Period 1	Period 2	Period 3	Period 4	Period 5	Period 6
BAC	300,000	300,000	300,000	300,000	300,000	300,000
EAC	300,000	300,000	295,000	295,000	290,000	287,110
PV	14,800	29,600	44,400	59,200	74,000	87,520
EV	9,167	18,333	28,500	42,133	56,767	74,576
AC	12,100	23,700	33,800	48,600	60,350	64,150
CV Cum	(2,933)	(5,367)	(5,300)	(6,467)	(3,583)	10,426
SV Cum	(5,633)	(11,267)	(15,900)	(17,067)	(17,233)	(12,944)
VAC	–	– 0	5,000	5,000	10,000	12,890
CPI Cum	0.76	0.77	0.84	0.87	0.94	1.16
SPI Cum	0.62	0.62	0.64	0.71	0.77	0.85
CPI Cur	0.76	0.79	1.01	0.92	1.25	4.69
SPI Cur	0.62	0.62	0.69	0.92	0.99	1.32
TCPI	1.01	1.02	1.04	1.05	1.06	1.01
IEAC CPI Cum	395,986	387,825	355,789	346,047	318,935	258,059
IEAC 80/20	410,523	402,944	371,935	357,094	328,840	268,999
IEAC CPI X SPI	631,878	611,607	535,426	466,435	397,435	291,715

Figure 9-7. Project Summary Bicycle Data through Period 6

From the data, notice that many of the WBS elements have not yet begun while others are already completed. For example, WBS element 1.3.1 (front wheel), has a cumulative EV of $15,600, which is equal to the BAC. Additionally, in this case, the cumulative AC of $5,000 is equal to the EAC. The combination of these two conditions generally implies that the required effort is complete. Also notice that finished elements, such as 1.1.1 (frame) always have an SPI of 1.0, however the cost variance at the time of completion remains. This is an important point. Finishing an effort with a cost underrun or overrun is not an opportunity to remove or add budget in order to mitigate the cost variance. The variance against the baseline must remain. Appendix D on Using EVM Data for Schedule Analysis introduces a time-based SPI that does not revert to 1.0 upon completion.

Figure 9-7 illustrates the periodic, cumulative data at the summary level of the project. This view is necessary to help understand project trends. In this table it is easy to see the change in the project's EV data (PV, EV, and AC); the change in the project's EAC; the trend of cost, schedule, and at complete variances including the associated indices; and the resulting forecast from calculated independent EACs.

Some points to consider regarding the data in Figures 9-6 and 9-7:

- Elements 1.1.1 (frame), 1.1.2 (handlebar), 1.3.1 (front wheel) and 1.3.2 (back wheel) have all been completed.

- There have been no changes to the BAC, which means that there have been no approved changes to the performance measurement baseline either from outside the project or within from management reserves.

- No contingency reserve held in undistributed budget has been used to handle risks under control of the project management team.

9.6.2 Graphical Analysis of the Data

In the following sections we will demonstrate a series of typical graphs to help display the earned value data and forecasts in quick and easy-to-read formats.

.1 Graphical Display of PV, EV, and AC

Figure 9-8 plots the cumulative values for PV, EV, and AC. Viewing the data in graphical form quickly demonstrates trends in the data, and displays the relationship between the data elements.

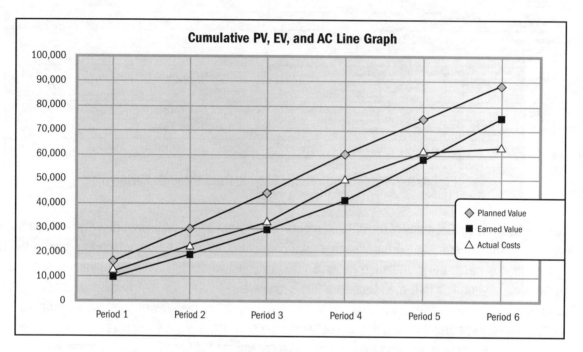

Figure 9-8. Cumulative Line Graph with PV, EV, and AC

For example, notice that the PV line is always above the EV line, meaning that this project has always been behind schedule. The "flattening" of actual costs in Period 6 is also apparent. This may be a legitimate trend, but it also should trigger an investigation to ensure that the costs have been appropriately recorded.

Figure 9-9 is another view of the project data which looks at the current or monthly data for PV, EV, and AC.

Looking at the current period data shows monthly values steadily increasing, with the exception of actual costs and, to a lesser degree, planned value in Period 6.

.2 Graphical Display of At Completion Data and Forecasts

Figure 9-10 graphically displays the independent estimates at completion (IEACs) that are reported at the bottom of Figure 9-7. The three IEAC methods are described in detail in Table 9-1, but all follow the same basic formula: AC + (remaining work/performance factor). The remaining work is BAC − EV. The three performance factors are: a) CPI, b) (CPI × 0.8) + (SPI × 0.2), and c) CPI × SPI.

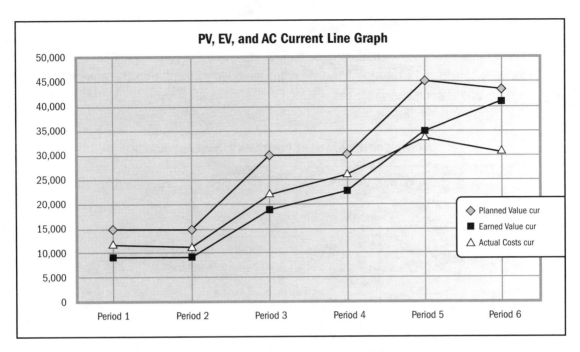

Figure 9-9. Current Data Line Graph with PV, EV, and AC

Figure 9-10 quickly illustrates that performance on the bicycle project has been improving steadily. As of Period 6, two of the three IEACs are projecting an underrun. In addition, the IEAC values demonstrate a clear trend towards the project EAC and the BAC, as there is a dramatic and steady improvement of statistical forecasts during the life of the project.

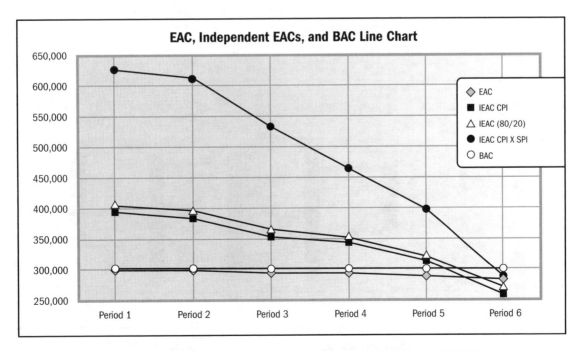

Figure 9-10. Line Graph with EAC, Independent EACs and BAC

.3 Graphical Display Project Variances

Also critical to the understanding of project status is the communication of project variances. Figures 9-11 and 9-12 represent two different methods of displaying the cumulative project cost, schedule, and at complete variances.

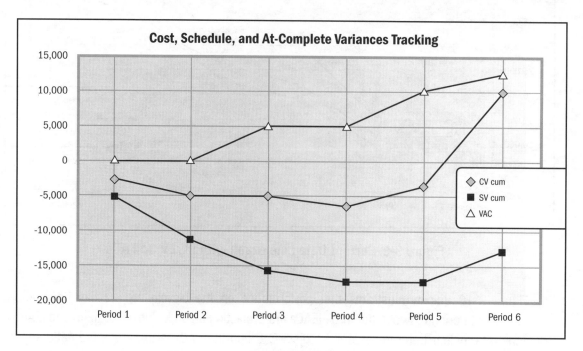

Figure 9-11. Variance History Line Graph

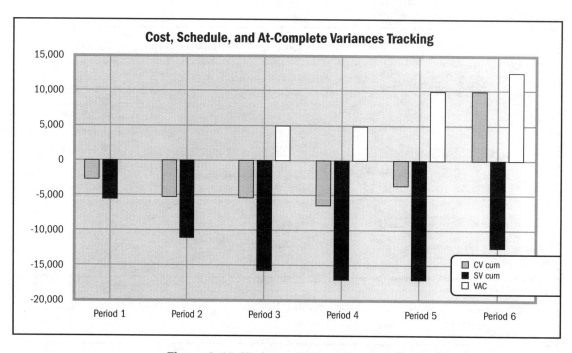

Figure 9-12. Variance History Bar Graph

Figure 9-11 demonstrates the variance trends, while Figure 9-12 better illustrates those variances that are above and below zero.

Another method of displaying project performance status is the bull's-eye chart shown in Figure 9-13. This graph displays the cumulative cost variance percentage versus the cumulative schedule variance percentage for all periods of the bicycle project. A bull's eye chart can also display CPI cum versus SPI cum to communicate the same information. The center of the graph is always CV% =0 and SV% = 0 (or CPI cum = 1.0 and SPI cum = 1.0).

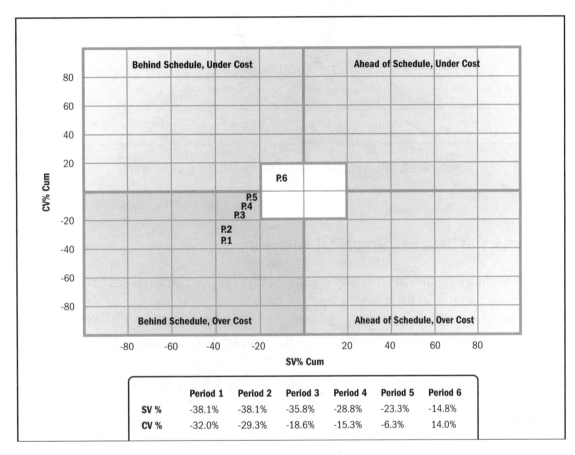

	Period 1	Period 2	Period 3	Period 4	Period 5	Period 6
SV %	-38.1%	-38.1%	-35.8%	-28.8%	-23.3%	-14.8%
CV %	-32.0%	-29.3%	-18.6%	-15.3%	-6.3%	14.0%

Figure 9-13. Bulls-Eye Graph Tracking Cost and Schedule Variances

The lower left quadrant represents a behind schedule and overrunning cost condition, which is where the bicycle project has been in Periods 1–5 (P.1– P.5) and shows that in Period 6 (P.6), the project has begun to underrun but is still behind schedule.

.4 Graphical Display of Project Indices

Figure 9-14 displays the project SPI, CPI, and TCPI indices. Notice that in Period 6, the TCPI dropped below the CPI. If this trend continues, the project team should consider revising the bicycle EAC.

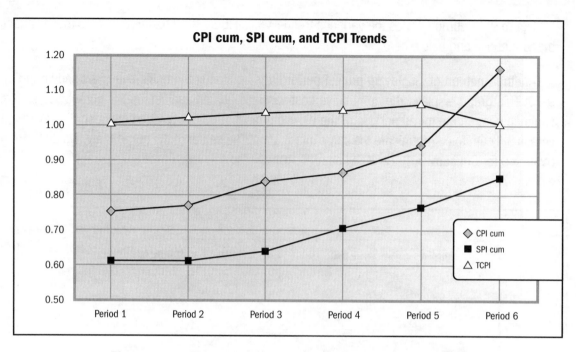

Figure 9-14. CPI, SPI, and TCPI History Tracking Line Graph

9.6.3 Summary of Data and Graphical Analysis

Even when summarizing the data into graphs and viewing the project performance trends, there is a great deal of information available. At the summary level, you can see that project performance has been improving; however the project had a fairly poor beginning. Looking at both the data in Figure 9-7 and the graphing of the data in Figure 9-9, it's obvious that the reason for the dramatic Period 6 improvements is a decrease in actual cost. Inspection of Figure 9-6 indicates that the largest cost underrun element is 1.3.1 (front wheel), where $15,600 of work was accomplished for only $5,000 of cost. The relationship between the CPI and TCPI is a meaningful measure of the validity of the EAC. As shown in Figure 9-14, the TCPI was consistently greater than the CPI until the last reporting period. And finally, independent statistical forecasts of project costs are finally coming in line with the project's own EAC.

The SPI is still below 1.0, but it is improving. It's important to note that the SPI is merely an "indicator" of the schedule condition. While it is an important and informative indicator, it does not take into consideration nor analyze critical path or logical relationships, and an SPI value at the aggregate level will not demonstrate important detailed activities that are not being accomplished. In short, it is advisable to use the SPI as an aggregate performance indicator, complemented with the use of the project schedule as the primary source for detailed scheduling information.

9.6.4 Management by Exception and Variance Analysis

Section 9.5.1 emphasized the importance of the "management by exception" approach, and the use of variance thresholds to help explain specific variances that are of potential concern and deserve management intervention. Figure 9-15 reports the cost, schedule, and at complete variances for each of the elements, plus percent complete and percent spent.

Bicycle Project Variances	Cost Variance	CV %	Schedule Variance	SV %	Variance at Completion	VAC %	Percent Completion (EV/BAC)	Percent Spent (AC/EAC)
Sum of WBS Elements	10,426	14.0%	-12,944	-14.8%	12,890	4.7%	26.9%	24.3%
1.1.1 Frame	-500	-12.5%	0	0.0%	-500	-12.5%	100.0%	100.0%
1.1.2 Handlebar	500	12.5%	0	0.0%	500	12.5%	100.0%	100.0%
1.1.3 Fork	0	0.0%	-2,000	-50.0%	0	0.0%	50.0%	50.0%
1.1.4 Seat	0	-	0	-	0	0.0%	0.0%	0.0%
1.2.1 Crank Set	0	-	0	-	0	0.0%	0.0%	0.0%
1.3.1 Front Wheel	10,600	67.9%	0	0.0%	10,600	67.9%	100.0%	100.0%
1.3.2 Back Wheel	650	6.3%	0	0.0%	650	6.3%	100.0%	100.0%
1.4.1 Braking System	-824	-70.1%	-2,744	-70.0%	-560	-4.9%	10.3%	16.7%
1.5.1 Shifting System	0	-	0	-	0	0.0%	0.0%	0.0%
1.6.1 Integration	0	-	0	-	0	0.0%	0.0%	0.0%
1.6.2 Assembly	0	-	0	-	0	0.0%	0.0%	0.0%
1.6.3 Test	0	-	0	-	0	0.0%	0.0%	0.0%
1.6.4 Checkout	0	-	0	-	0	0.0%	0.0%	0.0%
1.7.1 Project Management	0	0.0%	-6,400	-26.7%	-2,000	-2.3%	20.0%	19.6%
1.8.1 Engineering	0	0.0%	-1,800	-8.3%	4,200	5.3%	25.0%	26.4%

Figure 9-15. Drill-Down of Contributing Variances

For example, as of Period 6 the bicycle project is experiencing a $10,426 positive cost variance, $12,944 negative schedule variance, and a $12,890 positive variance at complete. A quick examination reveals that almost all of the positive cost performance can be isolated to a single WBS element: 1.3.1 (front wheel). In addition, almost half of the negative schedule performance is attributable to WBS 1.7.1 (project management).

Variance analysis shows one element, 1.4.1 (braking system), is both significantly overrunning and behind schedule. Based on the degree of the variances, this element would most likely exceed a variance analysis threshold and trigger a required explanation of the variances and further intervention. Such an explanation may take the form as shown in Figure 9-16.

Variance Analysis Report

Project	Bicycle				Report Period	Period-6		
Date	February 8, 2010				WBS Element	1.4.1 Braking System		

				Cost Variance		Schedule Variance	
	PV	EV	AC	CV	CV%	SV	SV%
Current Period	$3,920	$1,176	$2,000	($824)	-70%	($2,744)	-70%
Cumulative	$3,920	$1,176	$2,000	($824)	-70%	($2,744)	-70%

At Completion	BAC	EAC	VAC
	$11,440	$12,000	($560)

■ SCHEDULE VARIANCE

Problem Analysis – Cause
Several delivered components from one vendor have failed receipt inspection, resulting in approximately $3,000 of parts associated with the handle lever that were returned to the vendor for modifications. These parts were planned to be delivered by February 26, however they are anticipated to be returned on March 11. It is anticipated that the schedule variance will go to zero at that time.

Program/Task Impact
The braking system is on the critical path of the program. Delays in these deliveries may impact all downstream activity including the shifting system, integration, assembly, and test. The anticipated impact to the braking system is a 2-week delay in completion.

Corrective Action Plan (Include Expected Recovery Date)
The braking system team is working with the project manager and other component teams on a mitigation plan to recover some of the 2-week delay. Specifically, some component tests and product tests may begin without the braking system. In addition, we are working with the shifting system team to assess if activities can be performed simultaneously rather than serially as planned. Anticipate completion of the braking system by March 11, and program impact is still being managed and assessed.

■ COST VARIANCE

Problem Analysis – Cause
$560 of the cost variance is due to a higher than anticipated cost associated with the brake calipers and pads. The remaining $264 is labor associated with managing early receipt of wiring components.

Program/Task Impact
The $560 pad and caliper overrun cannot be mitigated and is included in the braking system EAC. No impact projected for the labor variance.

Corrective Action Plan (Include Expected Recovery Date)
The $264 of labor variance is level of effort activity performed earlier than anticipated. Since the associated wiring components have arrived early, these LOE activities will not have to be performed when anticipated in late February, and the $264 variance will go to zero at that time.

Impact to Estimate At Completion (EAC)
Purchase orders released to vendors for braking system parts, primarily the pads and calipers, were negotiated $560 higher than budgeted. Cost impacts associated with part inspection failures are still being evaluated, but a potential $1,500 – $2,000 EAC impact is possible.

Figure 9-16. Braking System Variance Explanation

9.7 Summary

The data on project performance is compared to the performance measurement baseline. The project management team can use PV, EV, AC, and BAC to measure current performance and predict future performance. The resulting measurements should be analyzed to understand what is causing variances. Depending on the cause of the variances preventive and corrective actions can be developed to keep the project performance aligned with the baseline.

CHAPTER 10

MAINTAIN PERFORMANCE MEASUREMENT BASELINE

10.1 Introduction

Maintain Performance Measurement Baseline is the process of managing changes to the project scope and maintaining the integrity of the performance measurement baseline. Figure 10-1 shows the inputs and outputs for this process.

Change in projects is inevitable. The project manager should expect that requirements will evolve, and so will the performance measurement baseline (PMB). Most projects, especially complex projects, will incorporate changes to the PMB at some point. Established rules exist within the context of earned value management (EVM) for dealing with these changes to the PMB.

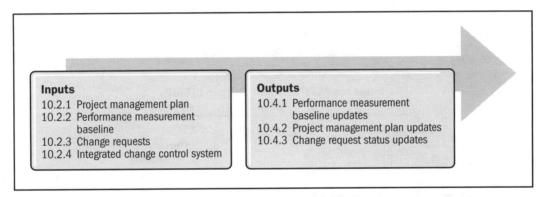

Inputs
10.2.1 Project management plan
10.2.2 Performance measurement baseline
10.2.3 Change requests
10.2.4 Integrated change control system

Outputs
10.4.1 Performance measurement baseline updates
10.4.2 Project management plan updates
10.4.3 Change request status updates

Figure 10-1. Maintain Performance Measurement Baseline: Inputs and Outputs

10.2 Inputs

10.2.1 Project Management Plan

The project management plan defines the processes used to execute, monitor, control, and close the project. Two important elements of the project management plan are the performance measurement baseline and the integrated change control process.

10.2.2 Performance Measurement Baseline

The performance measurement baseline (PMB) is the budget against which project performance is measured. It is formed by combining the budgets assigned to control accounts, summary level planning budgets, and undistributed budgets. It equals the PBB minus the management reserve. The PMB is maintained by project management, and all changes within the PMB are approved by the project manager. Figure 10-2, from *Earned Value Project Management*, Fourth Edition **[8]**, displays the PMB relative to the management reserve.

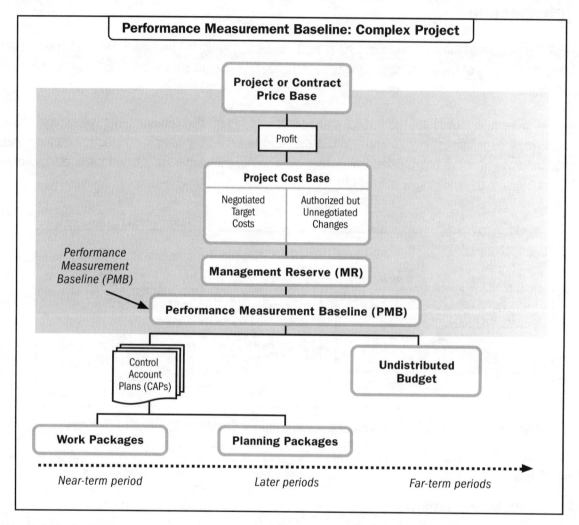

Figure-10-2. Relationship of Performance Measurement Baseline (PMB) to Management Reserve (MR)
(Source: Adapted from Earned Value Project Management **[8]**)

10.2.3 Change Requests

Change requests can be the result of project performance, an error in defining the scope of the project or the product, evolving requirements, a customer request, a change to a contract, a shift in the regulatory environment, or a change in the market. Changes to the PMB may occur because the existing budget or schedule is no longer realistic.

10.2.4 Integrated Change Control System

The integrated change control system is a formal process for evaluating project changes. Changes must be authorized, implemented, and communicated in a timely manner.

10.3 Description

10.3.1 Change Control Board Meetings

A change control board (CCB) is frequently used to analyze the impact of scope, schedule, cost, and other types of changes on the project and the performance measurement baseline (PMB). The only changes that are implemented are those that are approved by the CCB. On small projects, the project manager may act as the CCB.

Changes to the project or product scope impact the resources, schedule, and cost of a project. The change control process needs to account for the analysis which a scope change entails. Changes that do not impact the scope, such as changes to the schedule or the costs, still impact the PMB. The change control process needs to ensure that the integrity of the baseline is not compromised because of these changes or due to external dependencies that this change may impact.

10.3.2 Scope Change Analysis

All scope changes must be analyzed, the scope defined, and the impact on the control accounts assessed, including the need to add new control accounts or delete existing control accounts.

When new scope is added to the project, the PMB must be changed at the WBS level where the scope change will occur.

If new work is added to the control account, the new work should be placed into one or more new work packages. If an existing work package needs to be modified, it should first be closed, with the remaining budget plus the new budget placed in a new work package. In the latter case, when closing the control account, make the current budget (i.e., the cumulative-to-date planned value) equal to the earned value. This eliminates the schedule variance (i.e., no work remaining to be accomplished in the control account), but the cost variance is maintained at whatever value it has. Actual costs should not be changed for a control account that has begun and then is closed due to a scope change. Doing so maintains the historical cost variance, which contributes to the project's overall cost variance.

Often when scope changes occur, new control accounts are created. Although more rare, it is possible for the project to be de-scoped. In this case, unopened control accounts that are affected may be deleted.

At times the customer may initiate a change that needs to be incorporated into the project immediately, and the work should be planned and executed prior to negotiations on the pricing or cost for the change request. These types of customer-initiated changes are referred to as authorized but unnegotiated changes. In these circumstances, a firm commitment with regard to the price has not been agreed to by both the customer and the vendor. Typically, the customer will authorize work to begin and issue a letter with a *not to exceed* amount (NTE) (e.g., work is to be initiated, not to exceed $1 million) which authorizes the vendor to begin the work. After receipt of this letter, the customer and vendor enter into negotiations with respect to the cost for the requested change. In the meantime, the vendor initiates work and plans the new or revised scope that the customer has authorized. Where work can be executed immediately, the vendor initiates those efforts as well.

The portion of the authorized, but unnegotiated scope, which can begin immediately, can be distributed directly to the control account, and the PMB can be modified. However, typically, the bulk of the scope identified is for work not yet begun for downstream control accounts and work packages. In these cases, the remaining scope and associated value from the NTE letter are held in the higher level undistributed budget account.

As planning progresses to analyze the scope and associated budget, the remaining scope (or portions thereof) may be allocated to summary level planning packages. In addition, an analysis of new risks associated with the additional scope may be performed. Once risks are analyzed and risk management strategies crafted, the vendor may want to allocate a portion of the budget for management reserve to address any unforeseen risks.

Undistributed budget accounts should be resolved as quickly as possible, and the proposed scope provided in an NTE letter should be negotiated as soon as practical.

10.3.3 Cost and Schedule Rebaselining

A rebaseline equates to a major realignment of the PMB. The desired result from a rebaseline of the PMB is to improve the correlation of the planned work to the budget baseline, scope, and schedule.

The rebaseline takes one of two forms, listed below:

- Replanning involves a realignment of the remaining schedule and/or a realignment of the remaining budget to meet the original target.

- Reprogramming is a comprehensive effort to revamp the PMB. The result of this activity is an over-target baseline (OTB) or over-target schedule (OTS). An OTB includes additional budget in excess of the original budget allocation. An OTS occurs when the scheduled work and the associated budgets are time-phased beyond the original completion date.

The over target baseline is an acknowledgement that the current PMB cannot be executed within the current cost constraints. Essentially, the need for the over target baseline is an acknowledgement that the current PMB cost and schedule objectives are unattainable.

The OTB is an attempt to attain the project performance objectives in the context of new cost parameters. However, unless the causes for the cost variances are identified and rectified, the OTB will not be effective. All parties should focus on the conditions that led to the cost variances and agree on the proper corrective actions to take. In some instances, this may be recognition that the original cost objectives were unrealistic. For example, perhaps the original estimates did not account for the risk component of the estimate.

The over target schedule (OTS) acknowledges that the current schedule is unattainable and cannot be executed within the time frames required.

The OTS is an attempt to attain the project performance objectives in the context of new schedule parameters. However, unless the causes for the schedule variances are identified and rectified, the OTS will not be effective. All parties should focus on the conditions that led to the schedule variances and agree on the proper corrective actions to take. In some instances, this may be recognition that the original schedule objectives were unrealistic.

10.4 Outputs

10.4.1 Performance Measurement Baseline Updates

The result of the previous actions described in Section 10.3 is a new PMB. Once the rebaseline is completed, it needs to be formally accepted.

10.4.2 Project Management Plan Updates

When scope is added or deleted, the WBS and WBS dictionary need to be updated to reflect the change in scope. The risk register, cost management plan, and scope management plan may need to be examined and updated accordingly.

10.4.3 Change Request Status Updates

Changes that are approved are implemented and the corresponding project management plan components, PMB, and project documents are updated. Changes that are deferred or not approved are recorded in the change log along with the reason for the decision. Figure 10-3 displays a change log to record key information about the change request that affects the baseline.

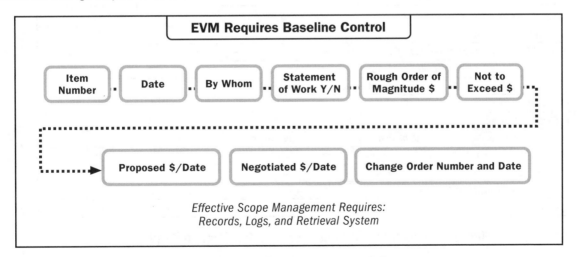

Figure 10-3. Example of Change Log for Recording Key Information About a Change Request Affecting the Baseline (Source: Earned Value Project Management [7])

10.5 Considerations

Baseline changes occur and need to be dealt with in a timely manner in order to make EVM effective over the span of the entire project. The goal is to maintain the integrity of the performance measurement baseline (PMB) so that measurements are meaningful. Changes to the PMB will cause changes to some unopened control accounts.

Work scope and budget, if moved from one control account to another, are always moved together. Budget must never be transferred simply to eliminate variances.

The cumulative PV can not be changed without changes to the scope and corresponding budget. Cumulative AC or EV cannot be changed either, except to correct prior errors.

When new scope is added, consider whether additional management or contingency reserves need to be added to the existing management or contingency reserves. How these reserves are treated relative to the PMB is addressed in Chapter 8.

10.6 Threaded Example for Bicycle Project

A customer-initiated and approved change request (see Figure 10-4) is received for the bicycle project. The impact is to one control account that has not been opened and work has not begun.

The change affects the first branch of the WBS at 1.1.4 (seat). The customer has requested that the material for the seat be changed from a polyester fabric to leather. The original schedule is shown in Figure 10-5. This

Change Request For Bicycle Project		
The change request below represents a customer-initiated change for the seat composition material from a polyester fabric to leather.		
Person Requesting Change: *John Smith*	Change Number: *001*	
Date: February 10, 20XX		
Detailed Description of Proposed Change:		
Change of material composition for the seat cover from polyester fabric to leather.		
Justification for Proposed Change: Customer Initiated		
Customer request		
Impacts of Change:		
The following documents will need to be updated as a result of the change request:		
☑ *WBS dictionary*		
☑ *Budget*		
☑ *Control account plan*		
☑ *Schedule*		

Figure 10-4. Example of Customer-Initiated Change Request

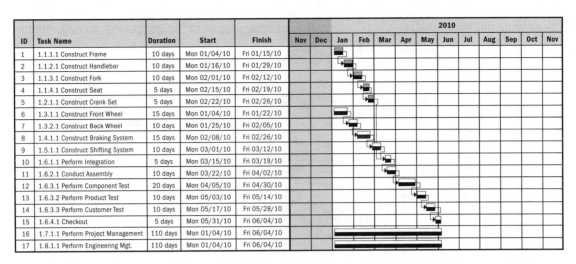

Figure 10-5. Example Showing Original Project Schedule

ID	Task Name	Duration	Start	Finish
1	1.1.1.1 Construct Frame	10 days	Mon 01/04/10	Fri 01/15/10
2	1.1.2.1 Construct Handlebar	10 days	Mon 01/16/10	Fri 01/29/10
3	1.1.3.1 Construct Fork	10 days	Mon 02/01/10	Fri 02/12/10
4	1.1.4.1 Construct Seat	5 days	Mon 02/15/10	Fri 02/19/10
5	1.2.1.1 Construct Crank Set	5 days	Mon 02/22/10	Fri 02/26/10
6	1.3.1.1 Construct Front Wheel	15 days	Mon 01/04/10	Fri 01/22/10
7	1.3.2.1 Construct Back Wheel	10 days	Mon 01/25/10	Fri 02/05/10
8	1.4.1.1 Construct Braking System	15 days	Mon 02/08/10	Fri 02/26/10
9	1.5.1.1 Construct Shifting System	10 days	Mon 03/01/10	Fri 03/12/10
10	1.6.1.1 Perform Integration	5 days	Mon 03/15/10	Fri 03/19/10
11	1.6.2.1 Conduct Assembly	10 days	Mon 03/22/10	Fri 04/02/10
12	1.6.3.1 Perform Component Test	20 days	Mon 04/05/10	Fri 04/30/10
13	1.6.3.2 Perform Product Test	10 days	Mon 05/03/10	Fri 05/14/10
14	1.6.3.3 Perform Customer Test	10 days	Mon 05/17/10	Fri 05/28/10
15	1.6.4.1 Checkout	5 days	Mon 05/31/10	Fri 06/04/10
16	1.7.1.1 Perform Project Management	110 days	Mon 01/04/10	Fri 06/04/10
17	1.8.1.1 Perform Engineering Mgt.	110 days	Mon 01/04/10	Fri 06/04/10

ID	Task Name	Duration	Start	Finish
1	1.1.1.1 Construct Frame	10 days	Mon 01/04/10	Fri 01/15/10
2	1.1.2.1 Construct Handlebar	10 days	Mon 01/18/10	Fri 01/29/10
3	1.1.3.1 Construct Fork	10 days	Mon 02/01/10	Fri 02/12/10
4	1.1.4.1 Construct Seat	19 days	Mon 02/15/10	Thu 03/11/10
5	1.2.1.1 Construct Crank Set	5 days	Fri 03/12/10	Thu 03/18/10
6	1.3.1.1 Construct Front Wheel	15 days	Mon 01/04/10	Fri 01/22/10
7	1.3.2.1 Construct Back Wheel	10 days	Mon 01/25/10	Fri 02/05/10
8	1.4.1.1 Construct Braking System	15 days	Mon 02/08/10	Fri 02/26/10
9	1.5.1.1 Construct Shifting System	10 days	Mon 03/01/10	Fri 03/12/10
10	1.6.1.1 Perform Integration	5 days	Fri 03/15/10	Thu 03/19/10
11	1.6.2.1 Conduct Assembly	10 days	Fri 03/26/10	Thu 04/08/10
12	1.6.3.1 Perform Component Test	20 days	Fri 04/05/10	Thu 04/30/10
13	1.6.3.2 Perform Product Test	10 days	Fri 05/07/10	Thu 05/20/10
14	1.6.3.3 Perform Customer Test	10 days	Fri 05/17/10	Thu 05/28/10
15	1.6.4.1 Checkout	5 days	Fri 06/04/10	Thu 06/10/10
16	1.7.1.1 Perform Project Management	110 days	Fri 01/08/10	Thu 06/10/10
17	1.8.1.1 Perform Engineering Mgt.	110 days	Fri 01/08/10	Thu 06/10/10

Figure 10-6. Example Showing How Change Request for Seat Affects Project Schedule

change results in an estimated $600 increased cost and an estimated 2-week schedule delay (see Figure 10-6). The PMB will need to be revised.

The existing budget for the new seat material acquisition work package is increased by $600 (the estimated increase due to the change in material cost). The leather material is estimated to cost an additional $600. With the change to leather material, the new budget for the construct seat control account is $5,000 (see Figure 10-7), and the time to acquire the leather material will take 2 weeks longer than the original baseline schedule. The customer was apprised of the schedule and cost impact, and agreed to the delay and increased cost.

All other work packages and control accounts are unaffected by this change request, aside from the impact of the schedule delay on downstream control accounts.

ID	Task Name	CPI	SPI	Method	Physical % Complete	EV	PV	AC	REVISED PMB
1	1.1.1.1 Construct Frame	0.89	1	0/50/100	100%	$4,000	$4,000	$4,500	$4,000
2	1.1.2.1 Construct Handlebar	1.14	1	0/50/100	100%	$4,000	$4,000	$3,500	$4,000
3	1.1.3.1 Construct Fork	1	0.5	0/50/100	50%	$2,000	$4,000	$2,000	$4,000
4	1.1.4.1 Construct Seat	0	0		0%	$0	$0	$0	$5,000
5	1.2.1.1 Construct Crank Set	0	0		0%	$0	$0	$0	$3,600
6	1.3.1.1 Construct Front Wheel	3.12	1	Physical Measure	100%	$15,600	$15,600	$6,000	$15,600
7	1.3.2.1 Construct Back Wheel	1.07	1	Physical Measure	100%	$10,400	$10,400	$9,750	$10,400
8	1.4.1.1 Construct Braking System	0.57	0.29	Weighted Milestones	10%	$1,144	$3,920	$2,000	$11,440
9	1.5.1.1 Construct Shifting System	0	0		0%	$0	$0	$0	$10,400
10	1.6.1.1 Perform Integration	0	0		0%	$0	$0	$0	$6,000
11	1.6.2.1 Conduct Assembly	0	0		0%	$0	$0	$0	$12,000
12	1.6.3.1 Perform Component Test	0	0		0%	$0	$0	$0	$9,600
13	1.6.3.2 Perform Product Test	0	0		0%	$0	$0	$0	$4,800
14	1.6.3.3 Perform Customer Test	0	0		0%	$0	$0	$0	$4,800
15	1.6.4.1 Checkout	0	0		0%	$0	$0	$0	$4,800
16	1.7.1.1 Perform Project Management	1	0.73	Apportioned Effort	20%	$17,600	$24,000	$17,600	$88,000
17	1.8.1.1 Perform Engineering Management	1	0.92	Apportioned Effort	25%	$19,800	$21,600	$19,800	$79,200

Figure 10-7. Example Showing How Change Request Affects Budget

10.7 Summary

This chapter provides detailed information with regard to the reasons why a baseline may change, the process for dealing with changes, and the project outputs once the changes take place. It is essential that the integrity of the performance measurement baseline be maintained in order to track project performance in a consistent manner.

REFERENCES

[1] Project Management Institute. 2008. *A Guide to the Project Management Body of Knowledge (PMBOK® Guide)*—Fourth Edition. Newtown Square, PA: PMI

[2] American National Standards Institute. 2007. ANSI/EIA-748-A-1998 *Earned Value Management Systems.* New York, NY: ANSI.

[3] Project Management Institute. 2006. *Practice Standard for Work Breakdown Structures*—Second Edition. Newtown Square, PA: PMI.

[4] Lipke, W. H. 2009. *Earned Schedule.* Oklahoma City, OK: Walter H. Lipke, p. 4.

[5] Project Management Institute. 2007. *Practice Standard for Scheduling.* Newtown Square, PA: PMI.

[6] Project Management Institute. 2010. *Practice Standard for Project Estimating.* Newtown Square, PA: PMI.

[7] Project Management Institute. 2009. *Practice Standard for Project Risk Management.* Newtown Square, PA: PMI.

[8] Fleming, Q.W. and Koppelman, J. M. 2010. *Earned Value Project Management.* Fourth Edition. Newtown Square, PA: PMI.

APPENDIX A

GUIDELINES FOR A PROJECT MANAGEMENT INSTITUTE PRACTICE STANDARD

A.1 Introduction

A PMI practice standard is characterized as follows:

- Each practice standard provides guidelines on the mechanics (e.g., nuts and bolts, basics, fundamentals, step-by-step usage guide, how it operates, how to do it) of some significant process (input, tool, technique, or output) that is relevant to a project manager.

- A practice standard does not necessarily mirror the life-cycle phases of many projects. However, an individual practice standard may be applicable to the completion of one or more phases within a project.

- A practice standard does not necessarily mirror the Knowledge Areas within *A Guide to the Project Management Body of Knowledge (PMBOK® Guide)*, although an individual practice standard will provide sufficient detail and background for one or more of the inputs, tools and techniques, and/ or outputs. Therefore, practice standards are not required to use the name of any Knowledge Area.

- Each practice standard should include information on *what* the significant process is and does, *why* it is significant, *how* to perform it, *when* it should be performed and, if necessary for further clarification, *who* should perform it.

- Each practice standard should include information that is accepted and applicable for most projects most of the time within the project management community. Processes that are generally restricted or applicable to one industry, country, or companion profession (i.e., an application area) may be included as an appendix for informational purposes, rather than as part of the practice standard. With strong support and evidence, an application area-specific process may be considered as an *extension* practice standard, in the same manner as extensions to the *PMBOK® Guide* are considered.

- Each practice standard will benefit from the inclusion of examples and templates. It is best when an example or template includes a discussion of its strengths and weaknesses. A background description may be necessary to put this discussion in the appropriate context. The examples should be aligned with the relevant information in the standard or its appendix and placed in proximity to that information.

- All practice standards will be written in the same general style and format.

- Each practice standard project will assess the need to align with or reference other practice standards.

- Each practice standard will be consistent with the *PMBOK® Guide*.

- Each practice standard is intended to be more prescriptive than the *PMBOK® Guide*.

APPENDIX B

EVOLUTION OF PMI'S PRACTICE STANDARD FOR EARNED VALUE MANAGEMENT

B.1 Initial Development: 2001–2005

Recognizing the need for global guidance on earned value management (EVM) beyond that included in *A Guide to the Project Management Body of Knowledge (PMBOK® Guide)*, the Project Management Institute (PMI) initiated its second practice standard project in 2001 and invited the PMI College of Performance Management (PMI-CPM) to assume a leadership role. PMI-CPM accepted the invitation and agreed to contribute both knowledge and financial resources to help make the project a success. It was agreed that the PMI-CPM Vice President of Professional Development, Dr. John Singley, PMP, would serve as Project Manager of PMI's *Practice Standard for Earned Value Management.*

During the first year of the project, a project charter was developed, team members were recruited, and a preliminary draft of the *Practice Standard for Earned Value Management* was prepared. The project team was comprised of about 30 PMI members, most of whom were PMI-CPM members. During that year, the team held several meetings and working sessions, and by the end of the first 6 months, the team had developed an outline of the practice standard. Small writing teams were formed and given the charge of preparing the first draft. By the end of the year, a preliminary draft of the practice standard was distributed to the entire team for review. A team meeting was held to gather and discuss recommendations.

Although the outline for the practice standard aligned it with the *PMBOK® Guide* and focused its content on those essentials of earned value that contribute to good project management, it was the opinion of most team members reviewing the preliminary draft that it went beyond the guidance provided by the outline and lacked the desired focus on essentials. The President of PMI-CPM, Wayne Abba, who agreed with the team's assessment of the preliminary draft, presented a compelling recommendation to return to the intent of the outline and align the practice standard with the *PMBOK® Guide*. The assembled team members agreed with this objective, but expressed varying opinions about the manner in which to achieve Mr. Abba's recommendation.

The project manager decided on a course of action: The two writing teams were asked to finish any remaining work on their drafts (without making any major revisions) and submit them to the project manager for editing. During the summer and fall of 2002, with the help of an independent, professional editor, the project team attempted to reshape and revise the preliminary draft of the practice standard. The results of this effort were not satisfactory; the edited practice standard appeared to mimic the structure and content of the *PMBOK® Guide*. It became apparent that a different approach was required.

At about this same time, the practice standard project team began to grow significantly, adding many new members who wanted to contribute to the development of the practice standard. (By February 2003, the end of the second year of the project, the team had grown to about 80 members; during the course of the project's third year, team membership peaked to about 145 individuals.) On the recommendation of the PMI Standards Manager, Mr. Steve Fahrenkrog, the project manager of the practice standard prepared an article for the March 2003 issue of *PMI Today*. This article reaffirmed PMI's vision for the practice standard and renewed the project team's commitment to realizing this vision.

To meet the challenge of writing a standard containing universal guidance for a global community of project management practitioners, a new and different approach was adopted: the project manager hired a ghost writer to prepare a series of drafts, which the members on the project team would each review. Capitalizing on the expert knowledge captured in the earlier drafts of the practice standard, in June of 2003, the writer composed a rough draft and distributed it to the project team for review. Comments and recommendations were collected from the project team's members. The writer revised the draft practice standard to reflect the accepted recommendations and, in August 2003, the project manager distributed this revised draft to the project team for review. This process was repeated four times. The third draft, completed in October 2003, was submitted to the PMI standards program team.

The third draft of the practice standard was revised by the writer to incorporate recommendations of the PMI standards program team, as well as recommendations from project team (which had expanded to include about 145 members). Throughout the entire review/revise process, a concerted effort was made to align with the vision for the practice standard and to focus on providing universal guidance for a global audience. In early January 2004, the project manager submitted the exposure draft to PMI, In February 2004, PMI posted the exposure draft of the practice standard on its website for a 60-day period of review by the project management community. PMI invited reviewers to submit their recommendations.

The exposure process, which included special invitations to independent EVM experts (who had not participated in the standard development process), yielded 280 recommendations. Four small project teams were formed to help with the process of adjudicating the recommendations. During the summer and fall of 2004, the standard's project manager and writer used the accepted recommendations to revise the exposure draft into the final draft of the practice standard. In October 2004, the project manager submitted the final draft to PMI for publication.

From the beginning of the project to its end, PMI recognized the challenge of developing the *Practice Standard for Earned Value Management* to provide project management practitioners with a better focus on the essentials of earned value management that apply to most projects most of the time. The best-known practice of earned value management matured over a period of 30 years in the United States and allied countries through its application on large defense systems contracts. Most of the literature on earned value management and most of its professionally active community is grounded in that experience. Guidance for the practice of earned value management, written and followed by that community, is comprehensive project management guidance with earned value seamlessly incorporated. PMI's challenge in writing this practice standard has been to transcend that experience, extract the essence of earned value, and align it with the *PMBOK® Guide*, so that it applies to most projects most of the time.

B.2 Second Edition: 2009–2011

In January of 2010, the *Practice Standard for Earned Value Management* (PS-EVM) update project committee received its charter from the PMI Standards Membership Advisory Group (MAG) and began to update the first edition of the PS-EVM published by PMI. The committee assembled for the second edition is comprised of individuals from five different countries and an even broader variety of backgrounds. The initial meeting was in March of 2010 where the committee examined the existing practice standard as well as comments and recommendations received during the previous review and publication cycles. During this meeting, the committee decided to take a different approach to the structure of the practice standard.

The first edition of the PS-EVM focused on providing a succinct overview. It accomplished that goal in four chapters: (1) An Introduction, (2) Basic Elements, (3) Performance Analysis and Forecasting, and (4) Guidance for the Use of Key Practices. For the Second Edition, the committee decided to move to a "process" approach to EVM. Rather than provide an overview of the subject, it was decided to address the developmental flow of EVM on a project. Much like the structure of the *PMBOK® Guide* itself, the role of EVM dramatically changes during the project life cycle. It was felt that the reader should understand that project data (EVM data) is the result of careful planning, organization, scheduling, management, and even compromise. Thus, in the current structure, the analysis of project data is not introduced until Chapter 9 (the second to the last chapter).

The committee had some overarching goals when developing the material of this standard. First, it was imperative that we did not create another standard similar to that used on U.S. Government contracts. Our intent was to create a standard for use by a much broader audience, both within and outside of the United States.

One topic that received a great amount of discussion during the second edition standard development was "reserves." Reserves were not addressed in the previous edition of the standard and we felt it was important to address the subject. There was a great deal of discussion and debate among the committee members on how to define reserves. The committee finally decided to recognize two distinct types of reserves: management reserve and contingency reserve. This distinction represents a foreign concept to many in the U.S., but is aligned with the *PMBOK® Guide* and the global audience is very comfortable with how the ideas are presented.

Another topic that required discussion was the treatment of scheduling and, specifically, earned schedule. Chapter 5 on Schedule Work is a relatively light treatment of the incredibly complex and important topic of scheduling. This is by design, as PMI's *Practice Standard for Scheduling* is a well written document which was in the process of being updated at the same time as the *Practice Standard for Earned Value Management*. The EVM committee worked closely with the project scheduling committee to ensure consistency in both practice standards.

In the previous edition, the concept of earned schedule was treated as "an emerging EVM practice," and an example was developed in Chapter 3 to explain the basic metrics and concepts. In the past five years this "emerging practice" has had an interesting path of emergence. With some exceptions, the concept was not adapted on U.S. Government contracts. However, when the content and structure of the second edition of this practice standard was presented at PMI's Global Congress in Ireland in 2011, and at the European

EVA Conference in Ghent Belgium, it was evident that earned schedule has gained strong support outside of the United States. Subject matter expert reviewers of the PS-EVM Second Edition from the U.S. insisted on exclusion of the topic with the same intensity that non-U.S. reviewers insisted on inclusion. A compromise was reached by giving a more complete coverage of earned schedule, but placing that coverage into an appendix where topics that are not necessarily core to the subject matter of practice standards are presented.

The topics for inclusion in the appendices of the *Practice Standard for Earned Value Management*—Second Edition were carefully chosen and reviewed by the core committee members. Appendices are treated differently by the PMI review process in that they are not released for consensus body review like the chapters, thus, the committee acted as the primary reviewers of this material. These appendices add valuable understanding to the practice of EVM. As stated previously, the practice standard was written to explain how EVM is used as a best practice on most projects most of the time. This goal is covered well in the ten chapters. In addition to Appendix D on Schedule Analysis Using EVM Data the core committee decided that the subject areas of integrating Earned Value with risk management (Appendix E), Deployment of EVM Systems (Appendix F), and EVM Pitfalls and Recommendations (Appendix G) would provide useful material for EVM practitioners around the world.

The goal was to provide the global community with a readable document that (1) explains the basics of EVM clearly and concisely for new practitioners and (2) provides a reliable extension for those who practice project management and those who want a more complete coverage of EVM than given in the *PMBOK® Guide*. The *Practice Standard for Earned Value Management*—Second Edition is intended to represent the basis for enhancing the practice of EVM by the global earned value management community as well as encouraging its increased adoption by project management practitioners and organizations globally.

APPENDIX C

CONTRIBUTORS AND REVIEWERS OF THE *PRACTICE STANDARD FOR EARNED VALUE MANAGEMENT*—SECOND EDITION

This appendix lists, alphabetically within groupings, those individuals who have contributed to the development and production of the *Practice Standard for Earned Value Management*—Second Edition. No simple list or even multiple lists can adequately portray all the contributions of those who have volunteered to develop the *Practice Standard for Earned Value Management*—Second Edition.

The Project Management Institute is grateful to all of these individuals for their support and acknowledges their contributions to the project management profession.

C.1 Practice Standard for Earned Value Management—Second Edition Core Committee

The following individuals served as members, were contributors of text or concepts, and served as leaders within the Project Core Committee.

J. Greg Smith, Chair
Eric Christoph, PMP, EVP, Vice Chair
Neil F. Albert
Lloyd L. Carter, PMP, CPCM
Anthony R. Corridore, PMP
Kym Henderson, RFD MSc (Comp)
Takeshi Ken Nishi
Alexandre Rodrigues, PhD, PMP
Cynthia Stackpole, MBA, EVP
Kristin L. Vitello, CAPM, Standards Project Specialist
Steve Wake, MA

C.2 Significant Contributors

In addition to the members of the Project Core Committee, the following individuals provided significant input or concepts:

Sean Alexander
Glen B. Alleman
Gay M. Infanti
Jeffry N. Isom

C.3 Practice Standard for Earned Value Management—Second Edition SME Reviewers

The following individuals provided their subject matter expertise to the draft of the *Practice Standard for Earned Value Management*—Second Edition prior to the public exposure draft review.

Wayne F. Abba
Robert Ameen, EVP
Linda Girdner
Eleanor Haupt, EVP
Jia N. Liu, EVP
Thomas M, Machak, PMP, EVP
Barbara C. Phillips, PMP, EVP
Carl Pritchard, PMP, EVP
Stephan Vandevoorde, Ing
Mario Vanhoucke, PhD

C.4 Final Exposure Draft Reviewers and Contributors

In addition to team members, the following individuals provided recommendations for improving the Exposure Draft of the *Practice Standard for Earned Value Management*—Second Edition:

Ahmed T. Abd El-Hameed, MBA, PMP
James Aksel, PMP, PMI-SP
Haluk Altunel, PhD, PMP
Eduardo Bazo Safra, PMP
Jonas Boijertz, PMP
David Bradford, PMP
Kameswaran Chandrasekaran, PMP
Ashutosh Dhanesha, MBA, PMP
Hans Elinder, MSc, PMP
Gloria E. Folle Estrada, PMP
Jose Eduardo Motta Garcia, MBA, PMP
Jochen Guenther
Samuel Hobbs, PMP
Karen C Jones, PMP
Ammar W. Mango, PgMP, CSSBB
Marino Martínez Miniño
Abdallah M. Mousa, BSc IE, PMP
Henry Lapid Nuqui, PEE, PMP
Crispin ("Kik") Piney, BSc, PgMP
M. K. Ramesh, BE, PMP

Mohammad Irshaid Y. Abu Irshaid, PMP, PMI-RMP
José Rafael Alcalá Gómez, PMP
Vijaya Avula, PMP, CSQA
Caroline M. Birog, MSE, PMP
Ravivarma Bhasker, V
Damiano Bragantini, PMP
Marcin Chomicz
Francine J. Duncan, MIEEE, PMP
Jon Fleming, PMP
Charles T. Follin, PMP
Robert C Grove, MBA, CAPM
Hisashi Hirose, PMP
Raj Kumar Jhajharia, PMP, SPE
Dorothy L. Kangas, PMP
Pedro Marques
Imad Mouflih, PE, PMP
Mike Musial, PMP, CBM
Barbara C. Phillips, PMP, EVP
José Angelo Pinto, MIS, PMP
Michael Reed, PMP

Edmundo Reyes Cuellar
Marcin Schubert, PMP, OCEB
Saulo Simpasa, MBA, PMP
Gurpreet Singh, MBA, PMP
Geree V. Streun, PMP, CSQE
Tracie Thompson
Davida Trumbo
Dave Violette, MPM, PMP
Thomas M. Walsh, MBA, PMP

Bernard Roduit
Sameer Siddhanti, MSc, PMP
Digvijay Singh
Paul Solomon, PMP
Mark A. Swiderski, MBA, PMP
Biagio Tramontana, Eng, PMP
Nageswaran Vaidyanathan, MTech, MBA
Atin Wadehra, PMP
Anthony E. Wojnar, PMP

C.5 PMI Standards Member Advisory Group (MAG)

The following individuals served as members of the PMI Standards Member Advisory Group (MAG) during development of the *Practice Standard for Earned Value Management*—Second Edition.

Monique Aubry, PhD, MPM
Margareth F. S. Carneiro, MSc, PMP
Chris Cartwright, MPM, PMP
Terence J. Cooke-Davies, PhD
Larry Goldsmith, MBA, PMP
David W. Ross, PgMP, PMP
Paul E. Shaltry, PMP
John Zlockie, MBA, PMP, Standards Manager

C.6 Staff Contributors

Special mention is due to the following employees of PMI:

Donn Greenberg, Publications Manager
Roberta Storer, Product Editor
Barbara Walsh, CAPM, Publications Production Supervisor
Quynh Woodward, MBA, Standards Compliance Specialist

APPENDIX D

SCHEDULE ANALYSIS USING EVM DATA

D.1 Introduction

While there are limitations to using EVM data for schedule analysis, techniques have been developed which allow EVM data to be used to augment and improve the effectiveness of overall project schedule analysis.

However, consistent with long-standing EVM practice, the network schedule remains the primary source of schedule analysis. Also consistent with EVM best practice, the resource-loaded, time-phased network project schedule, should strongly correlate to the performance measurement baseline (PMB) as a prerequisite to effective "cost-schedule integration."

The schedule analysis techniques utilizing EVM data should be used as a cross check to network-schedule-predicted durations and completion dates and to assist in identifying potential exceptions for further analysis and possible corrective action.

D.2 Average Performance to Date Versus Average Performance Required to Achieve Completion Date[1]

A long standing technique utilizing EVM data is to compare average historic schedule performance and compare to the future schedule performance required to achieve an estimated duration (ED).

The formulas are:

$$\text{Performance to Date (average)} = \frac{EV_{cum}}{\text{Periods to Date}}$$

$$\text{Performance Required (average)} = \frac{BAC - EV_{cum}}{ED - \text{Periods to Date}}$$

While averages may not necessarily reflect either current planned or actual performance, this approach enabled the comparison and analysis of past average schedule efficiency achieved from an EV perspective and a comparison to the projected future efficiency required to achieve an ED.

---

[1] Adapted from "Pocket Guide to Program Management using an Earned Value Management System." July 2009. Humphreys & Associates, Inc.

D.3 Estimates of Duration and the Completion Date

D.3.1 Work Rate Predictions[1]

Other long-standing techniques that have been used to predict an ED and the project completion date utilizing EVM data have been collectively known as the "schedule averaging" formulas. The generic formula is:

$$ED = \text{Time Now (periods)} + \frac{BAC - EV_{cum}}{\text{Work Rate}}$$

Then:

$$IECD = \text{Project Start Date} + ED$$

where IECD is the independent estimate of the completion date.

The work rates historically utilized as performance factors include:

- $PV_{(current\ period)}$
- $PV_{(average)}$
- $EV_{(current\ period)}$
- $EV_{(average)}$

Inspection of the formulas, in particular the performance factors historically utilized, reveal limitations with these techniques. When a project exceeds the planned duration (PD), the value of PV_{cum} equals its maximum value, the BAC. Therefore, in the case of $PV_{(current\ period)}$ after the PD is exceeded there are no further current period values of PV to utilize as a work rate. In the case of $EV_{(current\ period)}$ in the generally unlikely condition of zero EV being accrued in a period, the calculation also becomes indeterminate. The use of current period work rates as performance factors may produce volatile predictions over time.

However, all the work rates, with the exception of $PV_{(current\ period)}$ will produce predictions which converge to the final outcome achieved and range of predicted outcomes for the project duration which can be used for further analysis.

D.3.2 Predictions Using SPI[1]

An alternative approach, an independent prediction of project duration has been utilized using EVM data[2]:

$$EAC(t) = \frac{BAC/SPI(\$)^{[3]}}{BAC/PD}$$

where PD = planned duration.

---

[2] PMI. 2005. *Practice Standard for Earned Value Management.* Newtown Square, PA: Author.
[3] SPI($) is the traditional EVM SPI. The ($) suffix is used to distinguish from the earned schedule, schedule performance index (time) (SPI(t)) which is described later in this appendix.

This formula resolves to and produces the same predictions as:

$$IEAC(t) = \frac{PD}{SPI(\$)}$$

While these formulas will produce reasonable predictions of the final outcome for early and on-time completion projects, the limitations of this approach mimic the limitations of the predictive capability of SPI($). The mathematically inevitable reversion of SPI($) to unity at project completion will result in predictive utility being lost when this reversion commences as the predicted duration will revert to the PD. Predictive utility using this approach is also lost when the PD is exceeded in the case of late finish projects.

D.4 Time Variance Using Graphical Method

A longstanding method to determine a measure of time variance based on EVM data is the graphical method which projects the EV accrued onto the PV curve. This is accomplished by drawing a horizontal line from the EV curve at the status date to the PV curve and reading the time increment on the X (time) axis as illustrated in the bicycle case study in Section D11.2.

D.5 Earned Schedule

Earned schedule (ES), developed by Lipke in 2003,[4] extends the graphical method of projecting EV accrued onto the PV curve.

D.5.1 ES Concept

The ES concept as described by Lipke is as follows:

> The idea of Earned Schedule is similar to Earned Value. However, instead of using cost for measuring schedule performance, we would use time. Earned Schedule is determined by comparing the cumulative EV earned to the performance baseline. The time associated with EV, i.e. Earned Schedule, is found from the PV S-curve. This concept of projecting EV onto PV is not truly new. It is illustrated in many books dealing with EVM (including Mr. Fleming's book [Fleming, 1988][5]). The significance of using the Earned Schedule concept is that the associated schedule indicators behave appropriately throughout the entire period of project performance.[4]

The ES concept is depicted in Figure D1. While the example depicts time increments in months, ES works with the time increment of choice, for example, weeks if weekly EVM is being utilized.

The ES concept includes a time-based computation, called the earned schedule which calculates the time increment where the EV at the status date should have been accrued.

---

[4] Lipke, W. March 2003. Schedule is Different. *The Measurable News, REDUX,* Summer 2003.
[5] Fleming, Q. 1988. *Cost/Schedule Control Systems Criteria: The Management Guide to C/SCSC.* Chicago, IL: Probus.

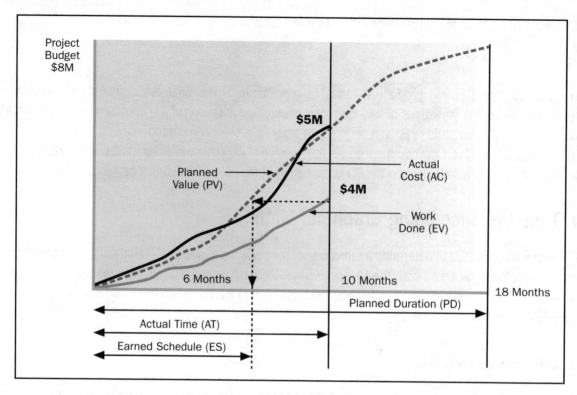

Figure D1. Earned Schedule Concept[6]

D.5.2 ES Indicators

From the ES calculation, a set of time-based schedule indicators are formed from the EVM data which behave in the same way as the EVM cost indicators:

Schedule Variance (time): SV(t) = ES − AT

Schedule Performance Index (time): SPI(t) = ES / AT

where AT is the actual time (in time increments) at the project status date.

When the ES exceeds AT, the SV(t) is positive and negative when it lags. The SPI(t) is greater than 1.0 when ES exceeds AT, and less than 1.0 when ES is less than AT. SV(t) will only revert to zero and SPI(t) to unity at project completion when the project completes on time.

The ES indicators, calculated by reference to the unconstrained actual time, behave appropriately and consistently as per the EVM cost counterparts for all phases of the project, including early and late finish projects.

---

[6] Stratton, Ray, 2005. Not Your Father's Earned Value. Projects @ Work: http://www.projectsatwork.com

---

D.5.3 ES Computation

The ES computation is expressed as:

$$ES_{cum} = C + I$$

where C is the number of *time increments* of the PMB for which EV is greater than or equal to PV.

I is the calculation for the fraction of the subsequent PV increment. The calculation is a linear interpolation using the following formula:

$$I = (EV - PV_C) / (PV_{C+1} - PV_C)$$

Using the example shown in Figure D1, the ES accrued is 6 months. The periodic measure of ES is derived from successive cumulative values:

$$ESperiod_{(n)} = EScum_{(n)} - EScum_{(n-1)}$$

where the subscript n is the number of time periods from the beginning of the project.

D.5.4 ES "To Complete" Indexes

The ES concept has been developed to provide similar metrics for the schedule to those provided by EVM for cost. The ES planned duration for work remaining (PDWR) is:

$$PDWR = PD - ES\ cum$$

where PD is the planned duration for the project.

To determine the future schedule efficiency required to achieve projected schedule outcomes, the ES "to complete" indices which are similar to the EVM TCPI for cost are:

$$TSPI = (PD - ES) / (PD - AT)\ \text{and}$$

$$TSPI = PD - ES) / (ED - AT)$$

where ED is the project manager's estimated completion duration.

The use of the TSPI for schedule analysis is similar to the TCPI for cost. Recent research indicates that, when the TSPI is greater than 1.1, the projected outcome (PD or ED) is also likely to be unachievable.[7]

---

[7] Lipke, W. 2009. The To Complete Performance Index—An Expanded View. *The Measurable News*, Spring 2009.

D.6 ES Completion Estimates

D.6.1 ES Completion Prediction[8]

ES provides two formulas for statistically predicting an independent estimate at complete time (IEAC(t)):

$$IEAC(t) = PD / SPI(t)$$

which is often referred to as the "short form" formula which is similar to BAC/CPI for cost and

$$IEAC(t) = ES\ cum + PDWR / PF(t)$$

where PF(t) is a time-based performance factor.

The latter is often referred to as the "long form" formula and enables the development and testing of PF(t) other than SPI(t) to ascertain where alternatives might more reliably predict project duration earlier in the project lifecycle.

From the IEAC(t), an independent prediction of project completion date can be calculated:

$$IECD = Project\ Start\ Date + IEAC(t)$$

where IECD is the independent estimate of completion date.

D.6.2 Future Performance

Consistent with the behavior of the EVM IEAC cost predictors, the ES IEAC(t) predictor projects the schedule future performance based on the historic schedule performance as represented in the SPI(t). Just as for cost forecasting, past project performance, while useful for initial prediction, may not continue into the future.

D.7 ES Analysis

Similar to EVM for cost, ES analysis is usually conducted as a "top-down" analysis process aimed at identifying adverse variances for further analysis and evaluation for corrective action.

Reliance on "high-level" ES metrics without further detailed analysis introduces the risk, which is the same as for EVM cost analysis, whereby lower-level positive and negative variances may be masked at the summary level.

As previously stated, the network schedule should remain as the primary source of schedule analysis augmented by the ES indicators and predictors.

---

[8] Adapted from Henderson, K. 2004. Further Developments in Earned Schedule. *The Measurable News,* Spring 2004.

D.8 Critical Path Analysis[9]

D.8.1 Introduction

The EVM data does not, in current practice, identify activities that form part of the critical path (or critical chain if critical chain scheduling is being utilized). Therefore, the network schedule should be utilized as the primary source for critical path analysis.

In practice, it has sometimes been noted that, when the project manager is actively managing activities on the critical path, the EVM (and ES) schedule indicators may indicate delay when the network schedule critical path analysis does not, or vice versa.

D.8.2 Critical Path Analysis Using ES

In addition to overall analysis of schedule performance, ES provides the ability to allow comparison to critical path performance. By treating the critical path activities (including completed critical path activities) as a separate project, the duration of the critical path can be forecast and compared to the planned duration as well as the overall project forecast.

From this comparison, the project manager can determine the relative performance of executing the critical and non-critical tasks and activities. If the ES metrics as applied to the critical path are better than the overall project ES metrics, this indicates that critical path is being protected and critical path activities are being properly prioritized during project execution. It may also be another indicator, provided that the critical path performance is sustainable during the execution of the project that the overall project ES metrics may improve over time.

Conversely, if the overall project ES metrics are less favorable than the ES metrics being applied at what is currently being analyzed and managed as the critical path, this may be a macro level indicator that the critical path has changed. Detailed analysis of the network scheduled is required to ascertain the actual status of the critical path and the critical path calculated project completion date.

D.8.3 Conclusion

These methods are recommended to further supplement the network analysis of the project schedule and the critical path.

D.9 "P" Factor[10]

D.9.1 Introduction

Following up from the development of the ES additional advances to practice have been developed. One of the most significant advances is the "P" factor measure of schedule adherence. In developing the tasks

---

[9] Adapted from Lipke, W. 2006. Applying Earned Schedule to the Critical Path and More. *The Measurable News,* Fall 2006.
[10] Adapted from Lipke, W. 2004. Connecting Earned Value to the Schedule. *The Measurable News*, Winter 2004.

and interrelationships between the tasks required to be executed by the project, the project schedule is also modeling the processes planned to be used by the project.

The "P" factor is a measure of the conformance of the actual process execution to the planned processes as embodied in the project schedule. It is important to note that that the "P" factor is not a measure of the efficiency of project execution. The "P" factor also provides, for the first time, important information on the sequence in which earned value has been accrued.

D.9.2 Concept

The idea of schedule adherence is embodied in the "P" factor measure. The "P" factor is the ratio of the EV accrued in accordance with the project schedule compared to the total EV. Therefore the "P" factor measure will be a value between zero (if schedule tasks are being executed completely at random) and one (if the conformance of the EV accrued during execution is perfectly aligned to the schedule).

ES facilitates the "P" factor calculation by enabling the identification of tasks in the schedule where work and EV accrued should have been accomplished in conformance with the schedule.

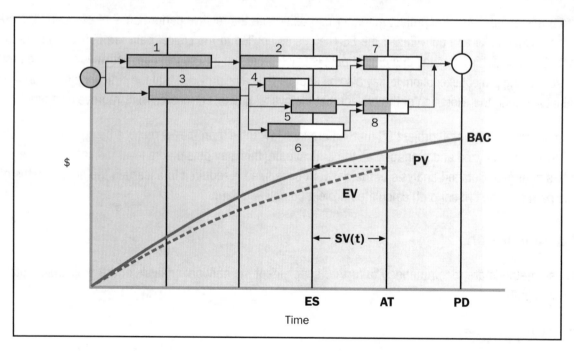

Figure D2. Relationship Between ES, PV, and EV[11]

---

[11] Lipke, Walt "Connecting Earned Value to the Schedule," The Measurable News, Winter 2004

To illustrate these points, the shaded tasks in Figure D2 represent the EV accrued at the status date AT. The ES line depicts the ES accrued at the AT status date. It is apparent that the SV(t) is negative indicating a project that is executing behind schedule in ES terms. It is important to note that the purpose of Figure D2 is limited to depicting the:

- Relationship between the network schedule and the PV curve (PMB)
- Distribution of the EV accrued on the project as at the status date, actual time (AT)

The shaded areas represent where work and EV were actually accomplished. If the project was executing in perfect conformance to the schedule achieving a "P" factor of 1, all of the shading that indicates a task completion would be to the left of and up to the vertical ES line. Therefore, only tasks 1 through 6 should be executed and have EV accrued. It can be seen from Figure D2 that:

- Tasks 2, 4 and 6 are incomplete and to the left of the ES line, and
- Tasks 7 and 8 have commenced to the right of ES line.

Therefore the process execution and EV accrued has not been achieved in complete adherence to the schedule.

D.9.3 Calculation

The "P" factor formula is:

$$P = \Sigma EV_j / \Sigma PV_j = \Sigma EV_j / EV$$

where the subscript "j" denotes the identity of the tasks from the schedule which comprise the planned accomplishment (i.e., to the left of the ES line).

The sum of the EV in the shaded areas of tasks 1 through 6 up to the ES line is the value of the numerator for P.

Notional data is used to further illustrate this. Where the sum of the EV accrued to the left of the ES line is $900 ($\Sigma EV_j$) and the total EV accrued is $1000, the "P" factor is 0.90 ($900/$1,000). This means that 90% of the EV accrued by the project has occurred in adherence to the project schedule. Conversely 10% of the EV accrued (to the right of the ES line) has been accrued out of agreement with the process sequence detailed in the schedule.

D.9.4 Impediments, Constraints, and Rework

The "P" factor construct also facilitates the development of additional useful information.

Where the difference between the EV − PV value for each task is negative, (identification can be automated) there is possibility of a process impediment or constraint impeding completion.

Examples of this from Figure D2 are Tasks 2, 4, and 6 which are incomplete and to the left of the ES line. Investigation by the project manager of these tasks with a view to implementing corrective action aimed at resolving the impediment or constraint is indicated.

Additionally, when the difference between EV and PV is positive, (identification also automatable), the task may be at risk of experiencing rework.

Examples from Figure D2 are Tasks 7 and 8, which have commenced and are to the right of the ES line. These tasks have commenced in advance of the schedule and with incomplete inputs from the preceding:

- Tasks 2 and 4 are incomplete in the case of Task 7

- Task 6 is incomplete, in the case of Task 8.

Tasks commencing with incomplete inputs are at risk of requiring rework after the preceding tasks are completed. This may also be evidence of poor process discipline, all of which indicate the need for investigation with a view to corrective action by the project manager.

D.9.5 Conclusion

This discussion highlights the benefits of ES and the "P" factor in facilitating analysis of the network project schedule by providing a list of tasks which can be used to prioritize the detailed analysis using the network schedule.

Furthermore, the "P" factor permits calculation of the EV accrued that is not in conformance with the correct process sequence. This facilitates the ability to forecast the rework resulting from out-of-sequence performance. The importance and value of maintaining the task precedence relationships in the network project schedule are also highlighted.

D.10 Summary

While EVM is oftentimes viewed as primarily being a method focused on project cost analysis and management, time conversion techniques to augment network schedule analysis have been a historic part of the EVM methodology.

Recent developments in the use of EVM data for schedule analysis, which is based on ES, has resulted in time-based indicators and predictors that parallel the EVM metrics for cost and can be used to further augment network schedule analysis.

The "P" factor measure of schedule (and process) adherence is an additional development which provides, for the first time, important information on the sequence in which EV is accrued.

Additional useful information obtained from the "P" factor includes the identification of activities which may be the subject of impediments, constraints, or "at risk of rework," which can be used to prioritize areas for analysis in the network schedule itself.

These developments further augment the core EVM claim and benefit of being a methodology which achieves cost-schedule integration.

D.11 Bicycle Case Study

This section extends the bicycle case study from Chapter 9 of this practice standard to demonstrate the application of the concepts presented in this appendix.

D.11.1 Average Performance to Date Versus Average Performance Required

To Achieve Completion Date

Table D1 assembles the periodic data, in this case weekly, and tabulates the average and required performance (using an ED of 22 weeks, which is also the PD) for the bicycle project as, at the end of Period 6, the status date in Chapter 9 of this practice standard.

While the average EV to date has been consistently less that the average projected performance required to achieve the ED of 22 weeks, the trend has been week on week improvements in the average performance and a reduction in the gap between actual and projected future performance required. This indicates progressively improving performance by the bicycle project since commencement.

D.11.2 Work Rate Estimates of Duration

Figure D3 assembles the periodic data, in this case weekly, and charts the estimates of duration utilizing the "work rates" for the bicycle project as at the end of Period 6, the status date in Chapter 9 of this practice standard.

The work rates utilizing the planned value measures (average and current period) predict project duration in line with the planned duration of 22 weeks. The EV performance factors predict a late finish project of around 30 weeks from Week 1 with progressively improving performance to an "on time" finish project (EV average) of around 22 weeks and early finish at around 17 weeks with the EV current period performance factor.

Table D1. Bicycle Project: Average Performance Data[12]

Period	Start Date	Period 1	Period 2	Period 3	Period 4	Period 5	Period 6
	4-Jan-XX	11-Jan-XX	18-Jan-XX	25-Jan-XX	1-Feb-XX	8-Feb-XX	15-Feb-XX
Performance to Date (average)		$9,167	$9,167	$9,500	$10,533	$11,353	$12,429
Performance Required (average)		$12,941	$13,132	$13,291	$13,272	$13,190	$12,896

---

[12] The units of measure in this table are of value ($) per period.

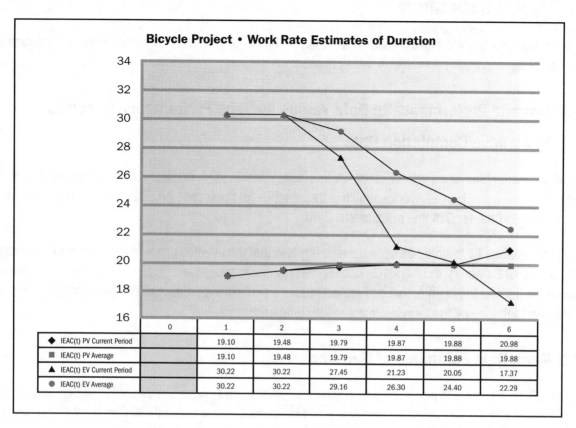

Figure D3. Bicycle Project: Work Rate Estimates of Duration

	0	1	2	3	4	5	6
◆ IEAC(t) PV Current Period		19.10	19.48	19.79	19.87	19.88	20.98
■ IEAC(t) PV Average		19.10	19.48	19.79	19.87	19.88	19.88
▲ IEAC(t) EV Current Period		30.22	30.22	27.45	21.23	20.05	17.37
● IEAC(t) EV Average		30.22	30.22	29.16	26.30	24.40	22.29

These estimates, consistent with all schedule predictions based on EVM data, need to be analyzed in conjunction with the network project schedule including the critical path and near-critical path activities. Analysis of the work rate performance factor that is most likely to best represent future schedule performance also assists in determining the best current estimate of project duration.

D.11.2.1 Time Variance Using Graphical Method Analysis[13]

Figure D4 shows the EVM graphical analysis of schedule delay as applied to the bicycle project. The time variance is approximately negative 1 week.

It has been suggested that the time variance be added to the planned duration to provide an EVM-based forecast of the schedule duration compared to the "planned earned value schedule."[14]

---

[13] Adapted from Fleming, Q. 1988. *Cost/Schedule Control Systems Criteria: The Management Guide to C/SCSC*. Chicago, IL: Probus.

[14] Fleming, Q. & Koppleman, J. *Earned Value Project Management,* 2nd Edition (Chapter 10). Newtown Square, PA: Project Management Institute.

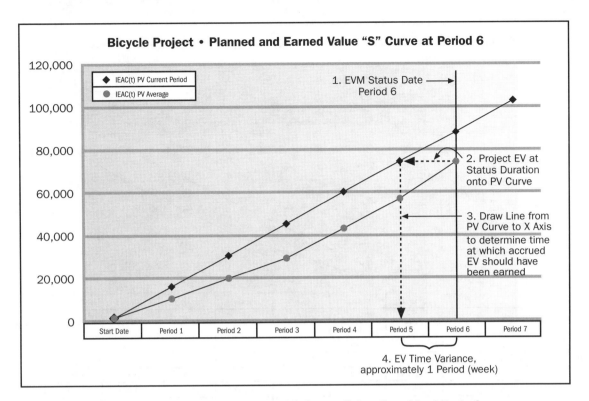

Figure D4. Bicycle Project: Time Variance Using Graphical Technique

D.11.2.2 Earned Schedule Analysis

Figure D5 assembles the periodic data, in this case weekly, and charts the planned schedule and earned schedule for the bicycle project as at the end of Period 6, the status date in Chapter 9 of this practice standard.

Graphically, it can readily be seen that the project is behind schedule with a planned schedule and actual time of 6 weeks and ES of 5.04 weeks. This results in an SV(t) of negative 0.96 weeks and SPI(t) of 0.84, both of which indicate a behind-schedule condition.

The IEAC(t) calculated using SPI(t) as the performance factor is projecting a period of project execution of 25.82 weeks with a corresponding IECD of 3 July 20XX compared to the baseline completion date of 4 June 20XX.

This analysis assumes, similar to EVM cost prediction, that the historic schedule efficiency as reflected in SPI(t) will continue into the future. In contrast to critical path method analysis which typically extends the project end date by the period of current delay, the projection of historic performance reflected in SPI(t) also explains the predicted delay at project completion of 3.82 weeks (IEAC(t) of 25.82 weeks minus planned duration of 22 weeks).

For the period ending 15 Feb, the TSPI indicator has been calculated by reference to an EAC(t) of 22 weeks (the planned duration). Its value of 1.061 suggests, as the value is less than 1.1 (subject to analysis of the network schedule and overall project) that the schedule delay may be recoverable if timely and effective corrective action is implemented.

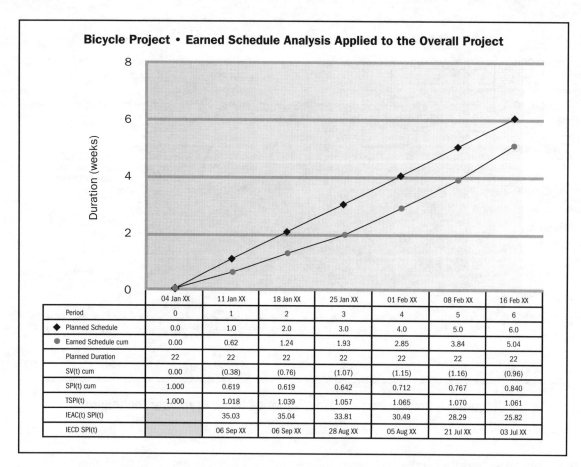

Bicycle Project • Earned Schedule Analysis Applied to the Overall Project

	04 Jan XX	11 Jan XX	18 Jan XX	25 Jan XX	01 Feb XX	08 Feb XX	16 Feb XX
Period	0	1	2	3	4	5	6
◆ Planned Schedule	0.0	1.0	2.0	3.0	4.0	5.0	6.0
● Earned Schedule cum	0.00	0.62	1.24	1.93	2.85	3.84	5.04
Planned Duration	22	22	22	22	22	22	22
SV(t) cum	0.00	(0.38)	(0.76)	(1.07)	(1.15)	(1.16)	(0.96)
SPI(t) cum	1.000	0.619	0.619	0.642	0.712	0.767	0.840
TSPI(t)	1.000	1.018	1.039	1.057	1.065	1.070	1.061
IEAC(t) SPI(t)		35.03	35.04	33.81	30.49	28.29	25.82
IECD SPI(t)		06 Sep XX	06 Sep XX	28 Aug XX	05 Aug XX	21 Jul XX	03 Jul XX

Figure D5. Bicycle Project: Earned Schedule Analysis for Overall Project

While the ES analysis of the bicycle project at the AT status date is indicating project delay, the trend analysis indicates that a significant improvement in project performance has occurred since commencement.

In Period 1, the SPI(t) of 0.62 indicated an IEAC(t) of 35.03 weeks which has improved to SPI(t) of 0.96 and an IEAC(t) of 25.82 weeks, respectively.

Determining the ability of the project to sustain the improvement in project performance to date into the future is ultimately a matter of detailed analysis of all aspects of the project. This should include the network schedule which may highlight future schedule constraints and technical performance measures that may also indicate future constraints to ongoing performance improvement.

D.11.2.3 Earned Schedule Analysis Applied to the Critical Path[9]

While the previous discussion applies ES analysis to the overall project, ES analysis can be applied to any area of interest within the project. This is achieved by treating the area of interest as a project in its own right for ES analysis purposes. The application of ES to the critical path (including critical path activities which have been completed) and comparing to the overall project ES metrics is a useful area for further analysis.

Figure D6 assembles the data for the bicycle project critical path technical activities (excluding engineering and project management).

Comparing the critical path versus overall project ES metrics at the end of Period 6 shows a slightly improved set of measures and indicators:

- ES of 5.29 for the critical path compared to 5.04 for the overall project
- SPI(t) of 0.882 compared to 0.840 overall
- SV(t) of negative 0.71 weeks compared to negative 0.96 weeks overall
- IEAC(t) of 24.6 weeks compared to 25.82 weeks overall.
- IECD of 25 Jun XX compared to 3 Jul XX overall.

These metrics indicate that the project manager is appropriately managing the critical path and prioritizing the allocation of work to critical path activities.

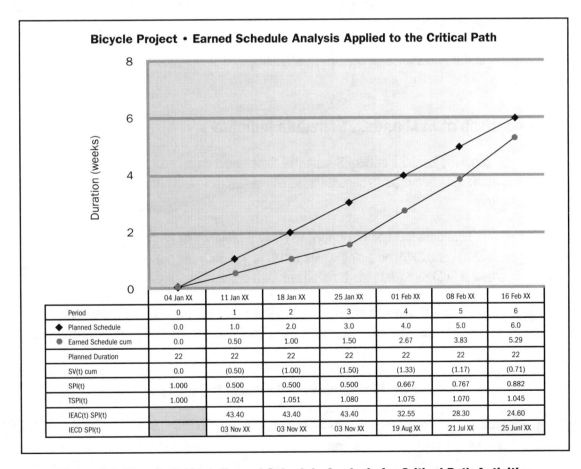

Bicycle Project • Earned Schedule Analysis Applied to the Critical Path

	04 Jan XX	11 Jan XX	18 Jan XX	25 Jan XX	01 Feb XX	08 Feb XX	16 Feb XX
Period	0	1	2	3	4	5	6
◆ Planned Schedule	0.0	1.0	2.0	3.0	4.0	5.0	6.0
● Earned Schedule cum	0.0	0.50	1.00	1.50	2.67	3.83	5.29
Planned Duration	22	22	22	22	22	22	22
SV(t) cum	0.0	(0.50)	(1.00)	(1.50)	(1.33)	(1.17)	(0.71)
SPI(t)	1.000	0.500	0.500	0.500	0.667	0.767	0.882
TSPI(t)	1.000	1.024	1.051	1.080	1.075	1.070	1.045
IEAC(t) SPI(t)		43.40	43.40	43.40	32.55	28.30	24.60
IECD SPI(t)		03 Nov XX	03 Nov XX	03 Nov XX	19 Aug XX	21 Jul XX	25 JunI XX

Figure D6. Bicycle Project: Earned Schedule Analysis for Critical Path Activities

Practice Standard for Earned Value Management — Second Edition
©2011 Project Management Institute, 14 Campus Blvd., Newtown Square, PA 19073-3299 USA

Provided the critical path performance is sustainable for the remainder of the project, which would need to be determined from analysis of the network project schedule, a slight (1 week) improvement on the overall project projected completion may be achievable.

D.11.3 "P" Factor Analysis

The "P" factor calculations for the bicycle demonstrate a very high level of conformance to the project schedule and the process adherence represented by the project schedule (see Table D2).

At the end of Period 6, 97.2% of the accrued EV has occurred in adherence to the schedule and only 2.8% of the EV accrued has occurred out of the correct process sequence. In addition, the trend since the start of the project has been progressive improvement in the schedule adherence achieved.

The estimated amount of accrued rework by Period 6 resulting from poor process adherence is estimated to be $565, with a forecast for the total amount of rework for the overall project equal to $2,263.

The benefit of the "P" factor is further illustrated by notionally reducing the "P" factor value so that, at Period 6, P equals 0.6. The recalculation of the estimated rework occurring from poor process adherence yields significantly different values. The estimated value for the accrued rework is $4,965 by Period 6, while the overall forecast for the project has increased dramatically to $29,216.

This demonstrates the importance of schedule adherence and being able to measure this performance characteristic using the "P" factor.

D.11.4 Comparison of EVM and ES Schedule Indicators

In order to fully show the benefits of the ES schedule indicators compared to their EVM counterparts, it is necessary to extend the bicycle project to become a "late finish project" and compare the respective EVM and ES schedule indicators.

The bicycle project EVM data has been extended to show a project that has completed seven weeks late. Figure D7 compares SPI($) and SPI(t) on a single axis which is generally the more useful for comparison while Figures D8 compares the EVM SV($) with the time-based SV(t) graphed on the second Y axis.

SPI($) and SPI(t) in Figure D7 shows a strong correlation up until the planned completion of the project in Week 22. In subsequent periods which is also roughly the final one-third period of project execution, SPI($)

Table D2. Bicycle Project: "P" Factor Calculations

Period	Start Date	Period 1	Period 2	Period 3	Period 4	Period 5	Period 6
	4-Jan-XX	11-Jan-XX	18-Jan-XX	25-Jan-XX	1-Feb-XX	8-Feb-XX	15-Feb-XX
P Factor		0.774	0.885	0.963	0.949	0.959	0.972

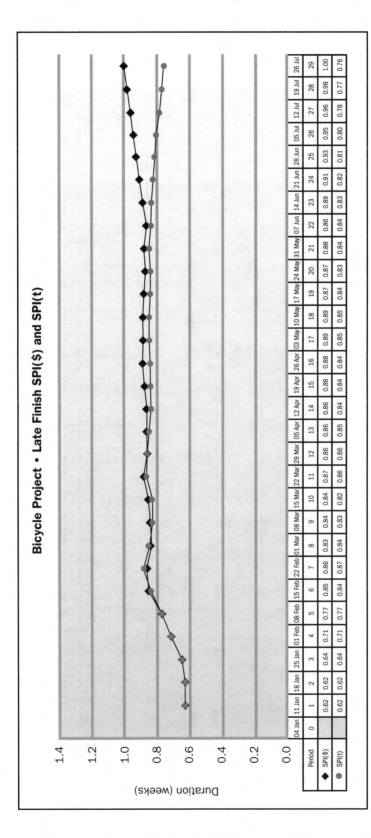

Bicycle Project • Late Finish SPI($) and SPI(t)

Period	04 Jan	11 Jan	18 Jan	25 Jan	01 Feb	08 Feb	15 Feb	22 Feb	01 Mar	08 Mar	15 Mar	22 Mar	29 Mar	05 Apr	12 Apr	19 Apr	26 Apr	03 May	10 May	17 May	24 May	31 May	07 Jun	14 Jun	21 Jun	28 Jun	05 Jul	12 Jul	19 Jul	26 Jul
	0	1	2	3	4	5	6	7	8	9	10	11	12	13	14	15	16	17	18	19	20	21	22	23	24	25	26	27	28	29
◆ SPI($)		0.62	0.62	0.64	0.71	0.77	0.85	0.86	0.83	0.84	0.84	0.87	0.86	0.86	0.86	0.88	0.88	0.89	0.89	0.87	0.87	0.88	0.86	0.89	0.91	0.93	0.95	0.96	0.98	1.00
● SPI(t)		0.62	0.62	0.64	0.71	0.77	0.84	0.87	0.84	0.83	0.82	0.86	0.86	0.85	0.84	0.84	0.84	0.85	0.85	0.84	0.83	0.84	0.84	0.83	0.82	0.81	0.80	0.78	0.77	0.76

Figure D7. Bicycle Project: Comparison of SPI($) and SPI(t)

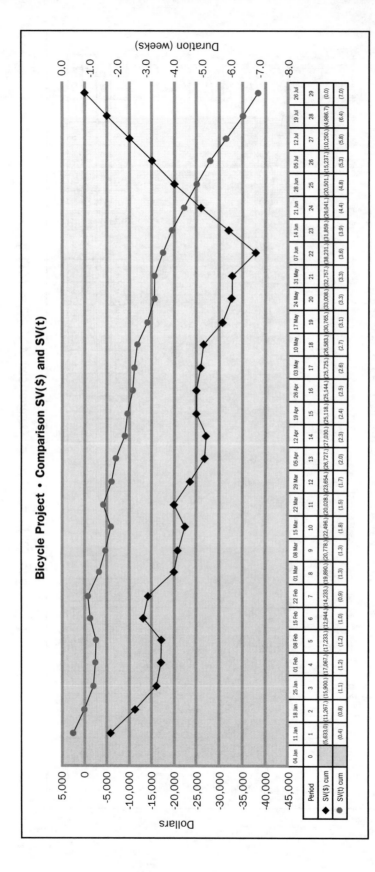

Bicycle Project • Comparison SV($) and SV(t)

Period	0	1	2	3	4	5	6	7	8	9	10	11	12	13	14	15	16	17	18	19	20	21	22	23	24	25	26	27	28	29
	04 Jan	11 Jan	18 Jan	25 Jan	01 Feb	08 Feb	15 Feb	22 Feb	01 Mar	08 Mar	15 Mar	22 Mar	29 Mar	05 Apr	12 Apr	19 Apr	26 Apr	03 May	10 May	17 May	24 May	31 May	07 Jun	14 Jun	21 Jun	28 Jun	05 Jul	12 Jul	19 Jul	26 Jul
SV($) cum		(5,633.0)	(11,267.)	(15,900.)	(17,067.)	(17,233.)	(12,944.)	(14,233.)	(19,890.)	(20,778.)	(22,496.)	(20,028.)	(23,654.)	(26,727.)	(27,030.)	(25,118.)	(25,144.)	(25,725.)	(26,583.)	(30,765.)	(33,008.)	(32,757.)	(38,231.)	(31,859.)	(26,041.)	(20,501.)	(15,237.)	(10,250)	(4,986.7)	(0.0)
SV(t) cum		(0.4)	(0.8)	(1.1)	(1.2)	(1.2)	(1.0)	(0.9)	(1.3)	(1.3)	(1.8)	(1.5)	(1.7)	(2.0)	(2.3)	(2.4)	(2.5)	(2.6)	(2.7)	(3.1)	(3.3)	(3.3)	(3.6)	(3.9)	(4.4)	(4.8)	(5.3)	(5.8)	(6.4)	(7.0)

Figure D8. Bicycle Project: Comparison of SV($) and SV(t)

loses predictive utility as it begins the inevitable reversion to unity at project completion. In contrast the SPI(t) values of less than 1 continue to show a project executing behind schedule.

The analysis of SV($) and SV(t) in Figure D8 is consistent with the EVM and indices. After Period 22, SV($) begins the process of reverting to zero at completion while SV(t) correctly shows the periodic actual delay experienced and the 7-week delay at project completion.

In addition to ES providing intuitive time-based schedule metrics, the improved utility of the ES metrics for portraying and analyzing schedule performance compared to the EVM counterparts is demonstrated.

D.11.4 Further Discussion Regarding Rework

Rework occurs from a portion of the out of sequence work that is not useable:

$$Rw = f(r) \cdot (1 - P) \cdot EV$$

Rework is performed over the remainder of the project at the rate:

$$\beta = Rw / (BAC - EV)$$

Using the rework rate at the beginning and end of a performance period the rework for period n can be calculated:

$$Rp\,(n) = \frac{1}{2} \cdot BAC \cdot (\beta n + \beta n - 1) \cdot (Cn - Cn-1)$$

where $C = EV/BAC$

The sum of the periodic values is the cumulative rework through period n:

$$Rcum\,(n) = \Sigma Rp$$

Using the Rcum and the present value of β, a forecast can be made for the total rework the project is expected to experience from the lack of schedule adherence:

$$RT = Rcum + \beta \cdot (BAC - EV)$$

Using the above formulas the rework for period six may be demonstrated:

$$Rw(6) = 0.813 \cdot (1 - 0.972) \cdot \$74544$$

$$= \$1697$$

$$Rw(5) = 0.862 \cdot (1 - 0.959) \cdot \$56767$$

$$= \$2006$$

$$\beta(6) = \$1697 / (\$277040 - \$74544)$$

$$= 0.0084$$

$$\beta(5) = \$2006 / (\$277040 - \$56767)$$

$$= 0.0091$$

$$Rp(6) = 1/2 \cdot \$277040 \cdot (0.0084 + 0.0091) \cdot (0.269 - 0.205)$$

$$= \$155$$

$$Rcum(6) = Rcum(5) + Rp(6)$$

$$= \$410 + \$155$$

$$= \$565$$

$$RT = \$565 + (0.0084) \cdot (\$277040 - \$74544)$$

$$= \$2263$$

APPENDIX E

INTEGRATING EARNED VALUE MANAGEMENT WITH RISK MANAGEMENT

E.1 Introduction

Earned value management (EVM) is a project management discipline that functions in concert with other disciplines and for which an integrated approach is essential. This appendix examines the relationship between EVM and risk management.

The relationship of risk and risk management with EVM is a complex one. We could even conclude that the reason for using EVM is to mitigate the risk of cost overruns on projects.

A risk is usually contemplated initially as an uncertainty. However, in order to be considered a risk, three elements are required:

(1) A possible risk event
(2) A probability of the event taking place
(3) An assessment of the impact that the risk event will have if it occurs

Without these three characteristics, only an undefined, imprecise uncertainty exists. This will be a crucial concept as we further discuss concepts in this appendix.

It is important to note that while risk and risk management are often thought of in terms of events that can jeopardize the project objectives, they can also be applied to those conditions that present opportunities for the project.

Strategies to deal with risks should be reflected in the performance measurement baseline (PMB). This may seem obvious, particularly in the case of risk management strategies, but past EVM practice and guidelines have often precluded the integration of the risk management. One particularly contentious issue has been budget for contingency plans.

A traditional view of EVM and EVM practice makes no distinction between contingency reserves for realized risks and management reserves, which, by definition, is for "in scope, but unforeseen" work. However, a compelling case can be made for the incorporation of contingency reserves as a component of the PMB in order to produce a creditable and realistic PMB.

E.2 Planning for Risk Management

In the initial phases of the project, organizations often will use statistical analysis to develop an S-curve (see Figure E1 below) that depict the project's range of potential outcomes based primarily on its assessed risks and opportunities. The statistical name for an S-curve is the cumulative probability distribution. S-curves are derived from the project's cost estimate, the cost estimating uncertainty, and the identified risks and opportunities, which are events that can cause the costs incurred to rise above or drop below the cost estimate. Each point on the curve indicates the cumulative probability (y-value) that the cost will be less than or equal to the amount shown on the x axis (x-value).

S-curves are often used to understand the range of potential costs for a program. This understanding enables business decisions. The final proposed, risk-adjusted cost estimate will be one that represents an acceptable business undertaking, given the organization's familiarity with the work, the assessed risk, the organization's risk appetite, and other factors.

E.3 Establishing the Performance Measurement Baseline (PMB) to Include Risk Management Strategies

When creating the PMB, the objective is to represent an executable, credible, and realistic time-phased budget plan and corresponding schedule. This plan, as represented by the PMB, is used to measure the actual project performance in comparison to the plan. Risk management strategies, particularly for risk mitigation, are included in the PMB.

Although, both project threats and opportunities represent risks, similar treatment can be made for those risks that represent opportunities and the strategies used to deal with opportunities. However, only the negative risks or threats will be dealt with in the remainder of this appendix.

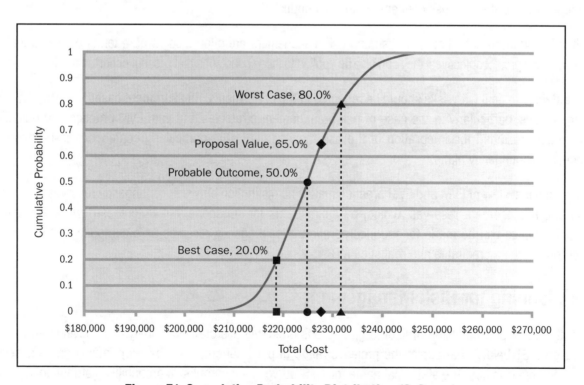

Figure E1. Cumulative Probability Distribution (S-Curve)

The risk management strategies for threats are:

(1) **Avoid the risk.** Instead of taking a course that may prove risky, we avoid the risk altogether. When the avoidance strategy is used, the time-phased budget for the method or path chosen are inserted when constructing the PMB, and the path "avoided" is not represented in the PMB. The tasks for the path chosen are also reflected in the integrated master schedule (IMS).

(2) **Transfer the risk.** In this situation, the threat still exists, but the risk is transferred in some way to another party. The time-phased budget associated with the risk transference, if any, is reflected in the PMB and the specific tasks are included in the IMS.

(3) **Mitigate the risk.** In this situation, the risk still exists, but the impact or probability of the threat is diminished in some way by proactively taking action prior to the risk horizon date. Although the risk is mitigated, residual risk remains. Usually, very few risks can be completely mitigated. Tasks to mitigate risks are reflected in the (IMS) and the time-phased budget for the mitigation is also reflected in the PMB.

(4) **Accept the risk.** The last remaining risk management strategy is to accept the risk. In some case, the risk poses a threat to the project objectives, but has a lesser risk ranking based on the impact and probability. The project manager and project team may choose to not actively manage this type of risk and thereby accept the risk consequences. The risk consequences are not worth the resources that may be required to mitigate it.

However, in some situations, there may not be a means to use any other risk management strategy, and, at times, this strategy is employed when other risk management strategies may prove too costly or are impractical. In these situations, we plan that should the risk event occur, a contingency plan is invoked. The contingency plan will address the risk if and when it actually occurs or if the horizon date for invoking the plan takes place. Should the risk not materialize, then the contingency plan is not invoked. As funds are needed to address the threat (or to exploit opportunities), the funds are drawn down from the contingency reserve budget. If the risk does not materialize, the funds remain in the contingency reserve budget.

Contingency plans and the funds needed to execute the contingency plans have not been consistently addressed for the most part and in some cases ignored in the EVM literature and practice. In many EVM texts, the budgets for contingency plans and contingency reserves either are not given separate consideration or are dealt with in the same manner as management reserve.

In the remaining sections, we discuss how the contingency budget is treated relative to the PMB.

E.4 Risk Throughout the Project Life Cycle

The integrated process diagram shown below in Figure E2 was developed by the (USA) National Defense Industrial Association Program Management Systems Committee's Risk Management Working Group (RMWG)[1], and subsequently published in the NDIA PMSC's EVMS Application Guide.[2] This diagram can also be found

---

[1] Defense Acquisition University (U.S. Government) web site (https://acc.dau.mil/CommunityBrowser.aspx?id=17609&lang=en-US)
[2] NDIA Program Managers' Guide to the Integrated Baseline Review

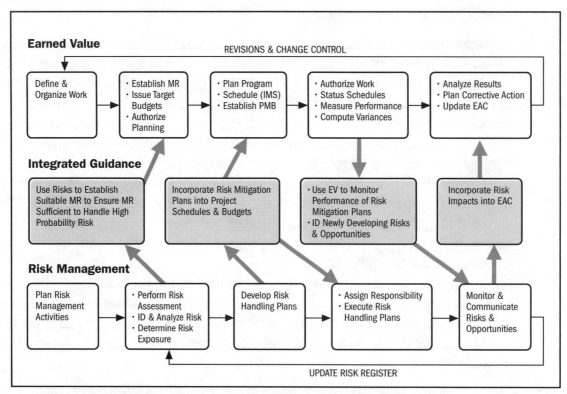

Adapted from the National Defense Industrial Association Program Management Systems Committee's EVMS Application Guide

Figure E2. Integrated Process Diagram

in Chapter 18 of the (USA) Government Accountability Office (GAO) Cost Estimating and Assessment Guide: Best Practices for Developing and Managing Capital Program Costs. The RMWG was a joint Industry/Customer team established to explore the integration of RM with EVM. The group's charter was to engage customer and supplier communities in the identification, collection, and sharing of requirements and processes necessary to integrate RM and EVM; the group subsequently published a white paper that established a business case for RM/EVM integration. The integrated process diagram depicts the risk management and EVM processes, the process interfaces, and the data that are shared between them to enable better planning, forecasting and decision making throughout a program's life cycle. There are multiple process interfaces and key data elements are shared to enable process integration; the arrows on the diagram depict the direction of the data flow from one process to another.

E.5 Establishing Project Reserves—Contingency Reserves (CR) and Management Reserves (MR)

Project reserves in this practice standard include both CR and MR. The distinction of these two reserves is described herein. An important distinction is that CR resides within the PMB and MR does not.

As a project is planned, both contingency reserves (to deal with identified risks that cannot be avoided, transferred, or mitigated and instead are accepted) and management reserves (to deal with uncertainties that cannot be quantified or specified) are included in the plan. An emerging practice is to include contingency reserves as a component of the PMB. It is suggested that contingency reserves are placed either within undistributed budget (UB) or a separate contingency reserve within the PMB. In order to maintain visibility of the overall risk profile of the project, it is also suggested these contingency reserves, not be allocated immediately to the control accounts, and instead reside in UB.

Management reserve, since its use is set aside for work that was neither foreseen nor defined in advance, is above the PMB. Contrast this with contingency plans that are crafted to deal with specific (and quantified) risks. Since specific plans have been developed, these plans can be incorporated into the appropriate control account. However, the funds to execute the plan are held in UB until either the risk or the risk trigger occurs. If this happens and the contingency plan is invoked, then funds are drawn down from the UB. It would also be acceptable to formulate a separate fund that is above the control account level and a component of the PMB called contingency reserve. For purposes of this appendix, we will only address UB, since UB is a recognized category traditionally included as a component of the PMB.

E.6 Contingency Reserves as a Component of Undistributed Budget

In many cases, particularly for large and very large projects, it is impractical to budget for each and every contingency. By the very nature of risk, it is unknown if the risk event will materialize. It is almost certain that some of the contingency plans will not be invoked and no contingency budget applied. The most common method of planning for contingencies is to sum the risk exposure for each of the risks with a contingency plan.

It is proposed that, for the budget, contingency execution reside in undistributed budget (UB). In this way, if the risk does not materialize, the budget for contingencies remain in UB until a risk does surface that results in a drawdown of the contingency budget. The earned value methodology is applicable because the contingency plan budget and tasks to deal with the prospective risk has been estimated prior to the execution of the contingency plan. Just as we do for any other components of a control account, we assess the planned time-phased estimate for the contingency plan versus the actual costs to execute the plan. Therefore, the integrity of the PMB is maintained. Since UB is a component of the PMB, no modification to the PMB is needed for application of the contingency reserve, unlike MR application, which would cause a revision to the PMB. Since a risk can be anticipated and a contingency plan developed, it is difficult to argue that the contingency was unanticipated, unlike the rationale for a management reserve budget.

When a risk does not materialize, those tasks are removed from the control account and not executed, and the contingency budget that resides in UB is never accessed. The contingency plan is not executed and the budgeted amount for the contingency is not allocated to the control account.

It is entirely foreseeable that at some future point, EVM and risk management will progress so that EVM recognizes a separate category for contingency reserve that is part of the PMB but not yet incorporated into the

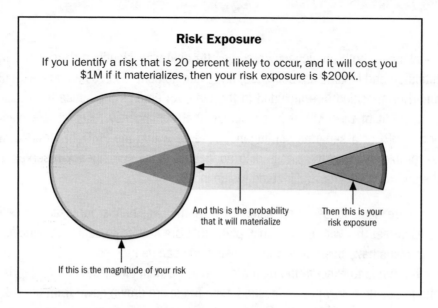

Risk Exposure

If you identify a risk that is 20 percent likely to occur, and it will cost you $1M if it materializes, then your risk exposure is $200K.

And this is the probability that it will materialize

Then this is your risk exposure

If this is the magnitude of your risk

Figure E3. Determining the Risk Exposure

control accounts, and is sitting at the same level as UB. However, until that occurs, the recommendation put forward is that contingency reserve is similar enough in concept to UB to include the contingency reserve in that category.

Figure E3 represents how the contingency reserve budget can be estimated for a risk. By aggregating the overall risk exposure for the total risks, we develop the contingency budget based on a percent of likely occurrence for any one risk. It would not be realistic to include in the contingency reserve an amount equal to the aggregate cost anticipated for all risks, should all materialize. Since the work associated with the contingency is known and the budget for invoking a contingency plan can be estimated, it would seem to differ drastically from the definition of management reserve, that is, unanticipated work that is within scope.

E.7 Integrated Baseline Review

E.7.1 Goals and Objectives of the Integrated Baseline Review (IBR)

An integrated baseline review (IBR) is an examination of the PMB encompassing the entire technical scope of the project. The IBR validates that the work is realistically and accurately scheduled, and that the proper amount and mix of resources (not the least of which is the budget allocated) have been assigned to accomplish all the project requirements. In this context, the IBR can, in and of itself, be viewed as a risk mitigation tool, mitigating the risks to the project objectives created by an unrealistic baseline that cannot be executed according to plan.

While this alone makes the IBR an indispensible and powerful tool, the IBR process also functions as a forum to identify project risks that may not otherwise have been identified.

The IBR concept and application of the process is a best practice that can be utilized to improve the prospects of achieving successful outcomes for all projects.

E.7.2 Goals of the IBR

The IBR seeks to develop an open and honest dialogue between the parties involved in the project, typically having a customer–vendor relationship.

Through this frank dialogue, both parties are able to examine the baseline and conclude that it is realistic and achievable or identify issues that must be addressed to ensure that the PMB it represents is achievable, provided that the baseline conforms to these stipulations. Because of this, in some circumstances, it may be desirable to conduct an IBR prior to awarding a contract. In assessing the validity of the baseline, control accounts (CA) are examined, along with the basis for estimating budget, resources, and schedule within the various CAs. During the IBR, the proposed earned value methods for determining progress toward completion of the CA will also be reviewed and agreed upon by both parties.

E.7.3 Objectives of the IBR

The IBR usually will encompass the entire project scope, although for certain very large, complex, multi-year projects, it may be decided beforehand to review an arbitrary percentage of the project scope (e.g., 90%). A review of the schedule will examine task sequencing and ensure that milestones and deliverables are organized in a logical and consistent manner. The manner by which progress is determined in the CA will be discussed to ensure that reports will reflect the progress achieved accurately. This focus is on the proper management controls to make the evaluation relative to the baseline.

In the course of conducting the IBR, certain risks will be identified which may impact the project objectives. Sometimes the risk takes the form of an opportunity which may produce a tangible benefit, although most risks will be in the form of obstacles to achieving a successful outcome. Other PMI publications focus on risk and risk management methods, and we will not duplicate those efforts in this practice standard. Technical solutions may also present risks, and the technical approach is also subject to review and discussion. This may result in the identification of risks not previously identified.

E.7.4 IBR Benefits

The IBR is perhaps the one activity that can be undertaken after the project is underway, which can lead to improving the prospects of the successful outcomes of the project, and lays the foundation for enabling a mutual understanding of the project risks. The customer and vendor in a contractual relationship each will benefit by understanding the other's perspective and expectations for the project. A properly conducted IBR will result in all aspects of the project management plan being understood and the PMB assessed for execution and performance. Resource needs are identified and accounted for in the project management plan. This serves to increase the confidence level of both parties in the validity of the PMB.

Known project risks are identified, and plans are reviewed for managing risks. Both parties understand the management approach for the project from their respective roles. The metrics and data that will be provided are agreed upon, and will serve as an early warning mechanism if the project strays off course.

After the IBR is completed, the project can move forward with the management by exception approach advocated by EVM, which provides improved traceability and focus.

E.7.5 The IBR Process

The IBR should be conducted in a cooperative, non-adversarial manner, between the customer and vendor for the purpose of validating the PMB. Where an organization has in-house projects, the IBR occurs between the project sponsor and the project team designated to execute the project.

When validating the PMB, the schedule, resources assigned, budget allocated, and other elements of the project management plan are reviewed. The intent is to determine if the project, as defined by the PMB, is realistic and executable.

The IBR is usually conducted after award of a contract. The IBR should be conducted as soon as the contractor has developed the PMB. At times, it may be advantageous for the customer to conduct an IBR prior to the contract award. In this scenario, the customer would narrow the competitive range to no more than, say, three vendors, using the other selection criteria. Then the IBR would be performed among those vendors remaining to select the best proposal.

E.7.6 Conducting the IBR

When conducting the IBR, the following activities are undertaken:

(1) Define the scope and schedule of the IBR
(2) Identify the appropriate team members to participate in the IBR
(3) Review the appropriate EVMS documentation
(4) Conduct training for the IBR team (both the customer and vendor)
(5) Document results from the IBR
(6) Identify risks and issues

E.7.7 Closeout of the IBR

Upon completion of the IBR, both parties should determine if the purpose of the IBR has been achieved. Has a mutual understanding been attained by both parties? For identified risks, has a risk management strategy been developed? Has the party or individual been designated that takes responsibility for the risk? Have new risks identified during the IBR been added to the risk register?

After the IBR closeout, the focus shifts to monitoring the actual project performance against the PMB. Deviations from the PMB could result in risks that require immediate management attention. Other project management functions such as appropriately updating the schedule, providing estimates to complete, on-going risk management, need to occur. Failure to perform these and other essential project management functions may in and of themselves create new risks impacting attainment of the project objectives.

E.7.8 Treatment of New Risks Identified During the IBR

When new risks are identified during the IBR, the risk management strategy is identified for each risk. Implementing the risk management strategy can result in a modification of the proposed PMB to account for mitigation, avoidance, and transfer strategies. This may lead to revisions in the proposed budget and the proposed project schedule. When the risk management strategy is to accept the risk and develop a contingency plan, this plan is incorporated into the project schedule. The contingency plan should result in a revision of the contingency reserve identified for the project.

Once all risks that are identified in the IBR are accounted for in the PMB, the parties may then validate the revised PMB.

E.7.9 Risk Areas

In the IBR, the risks associated with cost, schedule, technical approach, resources, and management controls should be examined. More often than not, the IBR will lead to the identification of new risks. These risks would follow the same process of quantification based on probability and impact, adding the risk to the risk register, and determining an appropriate risk management strategy. If this strategy results in new risk management tasks that need to occur, these tasks should be added to the schedule and an appropriate budget associated with the risk management strategy identified.

E.7.10 What the IBR is Not

Sometimes it is helpful in defining an activity to tell you what an activity is not. An IBR is:

    (1) Not an audit
    (2) Not a process review (not A CMMI assessment)
    (3) Not a graded event/test—No pass or fail
    (4) Not a change of scope
    (5) Not an EVMS compliance review
    (6) Not a vendor marketing opportunity for services or presentations
    (7) Not a basis for criticism

APPENDIX F

DEPLOYMENT OF EVM SYSTEMS

F.1.1 Introduction

Earned value management (EVM) has evolved to be a global best practice in performance management systems. The methodology is being applied across a wide spectrum of endeavors in many different nations and in many different industries. Yet, in any environment other than the U.S. Government, U.S. Department of Defense (DoD), and the defense departments of some other countries, guidance in the application of EVM is generally lacking. This appendix provides practical guidance to those individuals wishing to apply earned value management principles and methodologies, but uses a more results-oriented, rather than a process-oriented approach. It addresses the application of EVM systems from a project management life cycle perspective. That is, it applies project management principles to the application of an EVM system.

As mentioned in the first few chapters of this practice standard, there is a wealth of information available that defines and explains earned value management. This appendix does not seek to duplicate any of that information. Rather, it is written to assist those who are charged with establishing an EVM system (EVMS). The premise contained herein is that EVM is most effective when the EVMS is tailored to suit each organization's specific performance management environment, objectives, and goals.

To provide for an enduring application of an EVMS, an EVMS deployment must also take into consideration the cultural acceptance of the system. Such an approach best delivers the business benefits expected and ensures a continuing return on the investment applied. This appendix provides a framework within which to achieve those goals.

F.1.2 Success Factors—Performance Management Framework

F.1.2.1 The Framework

The framework and components for the application of performance management methodologies are illustrated in Figure F1. The three major components are leadership, methodology and cultural change. Note that EVM is just one of several performance management approaches that may be employed. Additionally, all of the approaches are driven by some perceived need to do so. The main body of this practice standard addresses the specific methodology of EVM. This appendix is concerned primarily with the other components of perceived need, leadership, and cultural change. These essential components deal with the culture of the organization. Further, they provide guidance to the organization on how to adapt the culture to embrace the chosen methodology. For our purposes here, we shall focus on employing the performance management framework components to implement earned value management not only through its unique methodology, but to embed the basic concepts of earned value management within and throughout the entire organization.

The adoption of any performance management methodology must necessarily be preceded by a perceived need to do so. The need is generally predicated on the belief that the system will prevent problems, enhance performance, or possibly overcome past deficiencies. For a perceived need to drive a new initiative, it must be visible, it must be compelling, it must be actionable, and it must be viewed as producing business benefits.

The successful transition of an organization's project management process to incorporate the earned value methodology is directly dependent upon the visible support it receives from senior organizational leaders. The methodology itself can be developed, documented, and rolled out to staff in a well-planned and executed deployment, but without a highly visible mandate and publicly stated expectations from senior leadership, the initiative is likely to flounder painfully for a very long time. The project management community will only embrace a new initiative if they see tangible evidence from senior leadership that the initiative is a business imperative. Senior leadership must clearly identify the expected new behaviors. If senior leadership expectations do not visibly change to the new paradigm, there will be little or no resultant change in tactical project management behaviors.

Performance management leadership is comprised of decision leaders, deployment (or implementation) leaders and methodology leaders. Decision leaders exist at various levels in the organization and are charged with managing the projects undertaken by the organization. They will use the EVMS to help them manage their projects. Deployment leaders are those individuals charged with the responsibility to manage the deployment of the EVMS. Methodology leaders, by virtue of their experience and expertise in the particular system being implemented, that is, EVM, are the subject matter experts who assist the deployment leader to successfully deploy the new system.

At the other end of the spectrum are cultural change enablers. There are six enablers:

- *Management involvement* drives the change, and without it not much changes.
- The system must be *user friendly*, that is, easy to use, intuitive, and simple.
- The system must *add value* to anyone who interfaces with the system.
- *Training and support* must be provided for the initiation of the system and to new staff as they join the project.
- As the system matures and changes over time with continuous improvements, *change management* processes must be applied to ensure that the changes are incorporated in an organized manner.
- Finally, the deployment of the EVMS itself must be treated as a project in and of itself. Thus, it must be managed with a *disciplined approach* consistent with project management principles.

Leadership will impose knowledge requirements on the methodology. The methodology will provide process discipline and information infrastructure, which through the cultural change enablers, promote cultural acceptance of the methodology. In turn, decision leadership receives valid and timely forecasts and feedback, which guide programmatic decisions.

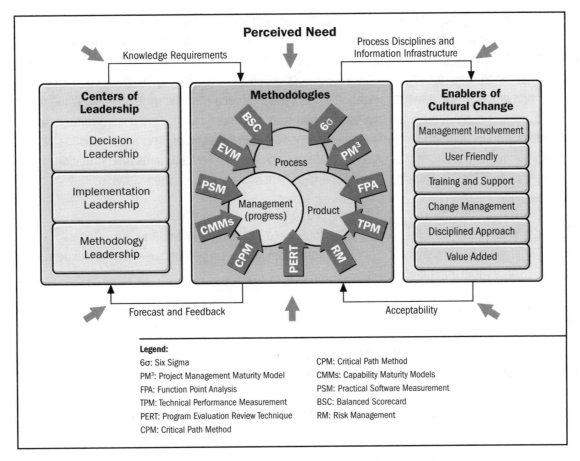

Figure F1. Performance Management Framework

F.1.2.2 Attributes of the EVM System

Earned value management (EVM) is truly a state of the art methodology for project performance management. Knowledge of EVM exists worldwide. Most commercially available project management software contains an earned value module. Nonetheless, in spite of its appeal, the use of earned value management as a disciplined, process-oriented, and sustained approach to project endeavors exists principally, in fact, almost exclusively, in those environments where its use is mandated by a buyer upon a seller that is providing project management services and products.

Earned value management is different from many of the other existing performance management techniques. EVM is a distributed, collaborative, inclusive (integrated) management system. For example, in a typical major construction project, the project control is frequently accomplished solely in the project management trailer located on the construction site with relatively little input from the hands on constructors, that is, those performing the work. When an EVM system is deployed, the performers must be included in the management process and, therefore, must take responsibility to plan and control and report on their portion of the program. Consequently, the performers, as well as the decision leadership, must understand and communicate performance using the earned value methodology. As a result, this mandates intensive training for everyone. Additionally, the system must be tailored to fit the organization's legacy infrastructure. It requires substantial bottom-up organization and operation, with top-down drive and oversight. In the absence of a customer-mandated requirement, an intensive, concerted effort must be employed. In such an environment, the key to success is molding the organization's culture to embrace the new methodology. While project need must drive project management system application and executive management involvement, and support must be visible, consistent, and real, it is the enterprise's culture that must embrace the usage of the system at all management levels. Lacking a customer mandate, commercial environments are particularly challenging. Constraining factors for deployment of a new management system include the following:

(1) It must use minimal capital resources to develop and deploy;
(2) It must use minimal operational resources to use and maintain; and
(3) It must be simple, comprehensive, understandable, and produce useful management information on a rapid and timely basis.

F.1.3 Initiating the Project

An initiative in a commercial enterprise, as in any organization, starts with an idea, a perception of a need. This need, if justified, will migrate to a business requirement by means of some institutional process and be developed into a formal requirement and justification for the allocation of funds. In most private enterprises, any substantial endeavor requiring allocation of funds is precipitated by a business case.

F.1.3.1 Developing the Business Case

F.1.3.1.1 Business Benefits

The initiation process must establish the business benefits of the project and relate it to the original perceived need. Further identifying the business improvement sought through EVM will validate the need and be the beginning of the business case. For an EVMS deployment project to provide enduring business improvement, the improvements must first be identified and quantified in the business case and then presented to management in a rational, objective manner. If this cannot be accomplished within the existing business constraints, there is little likelihood that management will embrace or be committed to the deployment. During deployment, the progressive achievement of the business benefits should be presented to management. Also, after a period of operation, the business benefits should be validated. Frequently cited benefits of EVM are:

(1) Better scope definition
(2) Accurate project estimating
(3) Thorough up-front planning
(4) Effective project accounting
(5) Accurate performance reporting
(6) Early identification and analysis of problems and risks
(7) Realistic forecasting

Simply stating these benefits does not generally result in management supporting the deployment. To gain their perception of the organization's current proficiency in attaining the cited benefits, decision leaders should be systematically surveyed. EVM needs to satisfy an identified business capability shortfall in order to gain senior management support. If management believes the organization is currently performing well in these areas, there is little to be gained by the deployment of an EVM system, and management will not support the initiative. Conversely, if there are known deficiencies, it is necessary to obtain management consensus of that fact. If such consensus exists, it can be effectively identified and clarified through structured interviews.

F.1.3.1.2 Scope

The EVM deployment project scope should be fully defined and documented to attain a comprehensive understanding of the work content and objectives of the project. The scope should address the project cost components in terms of the type of resources that will be required, for example, type of labor, material, other direct costs, and/or overhead resources. The manner of rolling out the system to projects, divisions, or departments should be clearly documented. The integration of performance management tools with the legacy infrastructure should be addressed. In addition, the identification of the standard of deployment that will be utilized to judge the acceptability of the deployment should be identified. The standard may an internal, national, international, or professional organization standard.

F.1.3.1.3 Schedule

The schedule contained in the business plan is the master schedule for the deployment effort. It should contain high-level pivotal milestones.

F.1.3.1.4 Budget

The budget should contain the sum total of the elements of cost that are identified in the scope. The cost associated with process development, tools, expert assistance, meetings, travel, and deployment of team labor should be identified to the maximum extent possible.

F.1.3.1.5 Priority

The deployment of an EVM system may require the involvement of many divisions within an organization. Business leaders need to endorse the implementation timeline and supporting resources. The deployment of EVM may coincide with other business change projects, and the respective priorities need to be clearly defined and agreed upon.

F.1.3.1.6 Organization

The organization section of the business case should identify the various roles and responsibilities to be assumed during the deployment, as well as operational phases of the system. This includes the executive steering committee, project management, system design, documentation and development, project control, and project performers.

F.1.3.1.7 Deliverables

The overall objective of the deployment project should be spelled out in a tangible and measurable way. One of the desirable attributes of implementing project management using an EVM system is that there are several discrete outputs that can be identified. These include the tools and products of EVM such as a work breakdown structure (WBS), a schedule, a performance measurement baseline (PMB), and performance reports, to name a few. The ultimate objective is an operating system which produces information that the decision leadership actively uses to make programmatic decisions.

F.1.3.2 Needs Assessment

A needs assessment is the process of identifying the difference between the "as is" and the desired "to be" of existing policies, processes, and practices. The assessment must address the cultural aspects of the organization as well as the documentation and infrastructure aspects. Specific needs assessment tasks include a review of the roles and responsibilities of various management levels and practices, and a review of documented policies, procedures, manuals, and other relevant documentation, as well as a review of the management infrastructure and supporting IT tools and practices.

F.1.3.3 Scaling the Application

This practice standard provides guidance about the EVM processes and practices that make up the totality of a disciplined EVMS. As the specifics of the deployment of an EVMS in a commercial environment can vary widely, the application of this practice standard's guidance must be tailored to fit an organization's individual needs. For instance, the management of internal projects is significantly different from the management of a contract-based project. A contract-based project requires all costs to be encapsulated for reporting, whereas it may not be possible or feasible to accumulate all of the costs of internal projects. Likewise, a construction project has significantly different management requirements than a software development project. Care must be taken to profile the EVM requirements to the individual situation from the beginning. To do otherwise would result in requiring adherence to requirements which have no management value, and this diminishes the cultural acceptance and business value of the system.

F.1.3.4 Project Bounds

A determination must be made of the extent and type of project to which EVM will be applied. For an organization that is yet to establish an EVM approach, the initial deployment may be used to prove its usefulness in one project, then spread to other projects within that organizational unit, and finally to projects at successively higher organizational levels throughout the company. A determination should also be made as to the size and/or type of projects that are considered amenable to the EVM approach. Another consideration is to determine at which point in the stage of the project life cycles when it may no longer be advantageous to apply EVM. Such determinations should be made in conjunction with the scale of the deployment as discussed in F.1.3.3.

F.1.4 Executing the EVMS Project

F.1.4.1 Performance Management of the Deployment Effort

The deployment of an EVMS is, in and of itself, a project with the full complement of project attributes. As a consequence, the management of the deployment should follow the applicable EVM principles delineated in previous sections of this appendix, scaled to the parameters of the specific deployment.

F.1.4.2 Leadership Aspects

The successful transition of an organization's project management process to incorporate the earned value methodology is directly dependent upon the visible support that it receives from executive management. The technique itself can be developed, documented, and rolled out to staff in a well-planned and executed deployment. However, without a highly visible mandate and expectation from executive management, it is likely to flounder. Before they will embrace it, the project management community will expect their management team to have determined that the earned value approach is a business imperative. If management expectations do not visibly change, there will be no resultant change in project management behavior. A major challenge for the deployment team is to obtain and maintain the executive management expectations. To this end, it is necessary to approach this challenge at the onset of the deployment effort by conducting structured interviews with executive management to ascertain their knowledge and expectation of EVM. The results of the interviews should then be presented back to executive management. Properly conducted, structured interviews are very effective in enacting the cultural acceptance of an EVM system.

F.1.4.3 System Design

The EVMS documentation should be merged into existing organizational processes and include a full life cycle depiction. Most organizations will already have a quality management system (QMS) in which their organization's policies and practices are documented, including their project management and governance processes. Such organizations must decide if they will blend the additional earned value methodology needs into existing process documents, write completely new and separate process documents, or construct a combination of both.

F.1.4.3.1 Story Boards

Within the resultant process document set, there should be an outline of the complete EVMS approach with clear identification of the responsibilities across the organization. This can be achieved through the development of a high-level process flow chart or "storyboard." The storyboard depicts the manner in which the EVM planning and execution documentation relate to each other and the responsibility roles (e.g., contracts, project manager, control account manager, project controller, etc.). This aids in the system design and provides an ideal training and communication device.

F.1.4.3.2 Focus Groups

The system design activity should not occur independently of the ultimate users. In order to obtain acceptance of the system by the project teams, the teams should be a part of the design effort. This can be accomplished by conducting focus groups where the system design draft is presented to the project teams for the purpose of obtaining their opinions and recommendations.

F.1.4.4 Training and Mentoring

As mentioned previously, EVM is a distributed, collaborative, inclusive management methodology. Its principles must be understood and embraced by all project management personnel and decision leaders. This can be accomplished both by formal classroom training and one-on-one mentoring. The mentoring should continue until each and every member of the team demonstrates a proficiency in the performance management tasks. Given that change is a predominant characteristic and change includes staff, training and mentoring is a continual process throughout the project life cycle.

F.1.4.5 Validating the Deployment

The deployment should be considered as accomplished when the objectives or deliverables, as contained in the business case, are obtained. EVM has a distinct advantage over alternative project management methodologies in that many of the outputs are tangible and measurable. But the most relevant desired output is a strong performance management culture with an involved and proactive management team.

Independent verification of the successful deployment of an EVMS may be desirable simply from an achievement standpoint or to enhance an organization's ability to declare performance management competency to existing or future stakeholders and customers. Verification may be performed internally by an EVM center of excellence, by personnel from other organizational units, or by external sources, such as customers or EVM consultants.

APPENDIX G

PITFALLS AND RECOMMENDATIONS

G.1 Introduction

Experienced project managers know there are associated pitfalls when EVM is not implemented properly.

The purpose of this appendix is to identify the most common EVM pitfalls and briefly describe some key recommendations as to how these pitfalls can be avoided. Practical experience demonstrates that if these pitfalls are properly handled, any apparent difficulties and hidden hazards can be overcome and the EVM method will deliver the expected benefits.

The main EVM pitfalls are grouped into the following main categories:

(1.) Lack of organizational support
(2.) Poor project controlling policies and poor quality of management response based on the EVM metrics
(3.) Poor project planning
(4.) Inappropriate cost and budget distribution over time
(5.) Inappropriate assessment of the earned value during work execution
(6.) Data consistency issues
(7.) Inappropriate consideration of risk management
(8.) Inappropriate modeling of subcontracted work
(9.) Inappropriate use of the base EVM formulas in "boundary" conditions
(10.) Inappropriate use of EVM for forecasting cost and schedule
(11.) Overreliance on the IT system/software
(12.) Inappropriate level of disaggregation leading to excessive data
(13.) Not using EVM at the portfolio and program management levels (e.g., for prioritization)

The remaining sections in this appendix address some of the most common pitfalls within each of these categories.

G.2 Lack of Organizational Support

It is crucial that the essential foundations of EVM are known and understood throughout the organization. The concept of a complex set of formulas and advanced metrics must be replaced by the straightforward need for a very essential set of measurements that deliver effective guidance to managerial control.

The EVM metrics must be used primarily to guide and help the organizational resources in achieving the objectives, and even function as the basis for incentives related to performance.

The indications, trends, forecasts and qualitative suggestions that can be derived from the EVM system, must be understood as solid objective ground for managers to make better decisions, and not as decisions themselves or as a prediction of the inevitable future.

Confining the knowledge about the EVM method to only specialized experts within the organization will tend to create fears and rejection by the organizational resources who feel the performance of their work is under constant auditing. Over reliance on the output produced by the EVM system, with little or no space for debate about the causes and interpretation, will lead to negative results.

Above all, EVM should be positioned within the organization as a common language to speak objectively about the performance of projects and to work as a basis for better informed decisions at all levels in the organization.

G.3 Poor Project Controlling Policies and Poor Quality of Management Response Based on EVM Metrics

While the original purpose of EVM is to deliver an objective description of a project's performance, it will only be useful if it leads to better control decisions. Using monitoring information to lead to effective decisions that positively influence the project future is essential.

This requires project control policies based on EVM metrics to guide management responses. These policies are developed by identifying patterns that relate to project status, responses, and their impacts, as well as the recording of lessons learned and, ultimately, by developing a knowledge management system.

Incorrect interpretations and over simplistic decision-making rules based on EVM results, can lead to a scenario of poor project performance and the lack of credibility.

G.4 Poor Project Planning (WBS—Scope, Scheduling, Estimating, Procurement/Contracting)

A well-known benefit of the EVM method is the discipline that it brings to project planning. In fact, without a set of planning requirements, EVM cannot be properly implemented.

These requirements are described in the main chapters of this practice standard and include:

- Proper decomposition of the project WBS to deal with a number of factors like uncertainty, risk, progress measurement, and accountability

- Proper scheduling to ensure a correct distribution of the project work, resources, and budget over time

- Proper estimating to deliver realistic targets of cost and schedule, against which performance can be meaningfully measured

- Proper consideration of subcontracted work with regard to scope definition, scheduling, and budgeting (as also discussed later in this appendix).

When these requirements are not observed and EVM is implemented on top of poor quality project plans, the outcome can be misguided results or difficulty in implementing EVM. Often in these cases, EVM is referred to as "not being applicable to this type of project or incompatible with this type of environment."

G.5 Inappropriate Cost and Budget Distribution Over-Time

EVM is based on the integration of scope, cost, and time and, therefore, it deals with the distribution of both the baseline budget and the actual cost over the planned and actual durations of the project.

The distribution of the baseline budget over the life of the project (i.e., PV—the planned value) will determine the rate at which the work is planned to be accomplished, and it is also the basis for evaluating the cumulative work accomplished (i.e., EV—the earned value). In turn, the recording of the actual costs incurred in the project due to resource consumption over time will determine the cost of the work performed (i.e., AC—the actual cost).

The comparison of the metrics PV, EV, and AC over time is the basis of performance measurement in EVM. If the project budget and the actual costs are not properly allocated to the correct time periods to which they refer to, the consequence will be incorrect performance and variance measures, which will misguide management and will be of little or no use.

The key principles for a correct allocation of budget and cost over time are as follows:

- *Baseline Budget*—The baseline budget must be allocated to the time periods where the corresponding resources are planned to be consumed as a consequence of work execution;

- *Actual Cost Incurred*:
   - Actual costs are allocated to the time periods where the scope that consumed the resources was executed (and not when the resources were invoiced or paid for)
   - Actual cost are calculated based on the real unitary cost of the resources (and not based on the unitary cost considered for the baseline budget)
   - Indirect costs require proper cost accounting procedures be employed (especially if these costs are of considerable magnitude).

There are some typical situations where an incorrect time allocation of the budget and cost may occur.

G.5.1 Excess of Level-of-Effort Work Packages

Level-of-effort (LOE) packages distribute the cost uniformly over the time period of the work package. LOE work packages exhibit a performance "as planned" (cost or schedule). If this method for crediting EV is used extensively, the real project performance will tend to be disguised by an "as-planned" performance tendency. Therefore, the LOE method should only be applied to those work packages that, in essence, represent ongoing work within the project (e.g., technical supervision or management monitoring). LOE must not be used to overcome practical difficulties in implementing the correct method to credit EV.

G.5.2 Discrete Allocation of Large Costs

There are situations where some work packages will consume very expensive resources that are acquired for the project at specific moments in time (a typical example is the acquisition of industrial equipment). If such large costs are allocated discretely to a specific time period (e.g., day, week, or even month), this will generate a sudden steep increase in both planned (PV) or actual work progress (EV), as well as in the actual costs (AC). This has a number of disadvantages either by "diluting" relevant performance variation, or by generating extremely high variations in the EVM performance measures that do not reflect the true performance of the project. Therefore, proper cost accounting techniques should be used to correctly distribute the baseline budget and the actual cost of the resources throughout the project scope.

G.5.3 Spread of PV Over Time Not Consistent with How EV is Credited

The way in which the baseline budget of a work package is spread throughout its planned time period (i.e., the PV) reflects the rate at which the work is expected to be executed. On the other hand, the method chosen in planning to credit EV will affect the way in which the actual work rate will be measured during execution. As an example, the LOE method will report a constant rate of execution, whereas the 25%/75% rule will report a step change in scope accomplishment. Therefore, if the distribution of the baseline budget over time does not take into account the method chosen to credit EV, false schedule variances will be reported (e.g., planning a uniform distribution in PV with a 50%/50% method being used to credit EV).

G.5.4 Difference Between Cash-Flow and Resource Consumption in Estimating AC

The AC metric is intended to measure the actual cost of the work performed. The cost being measured should relate to the *resources consumed* by the *scope accomplished* to date. This concept of resource consumption is different than cash flow costs, either invoices or actual payments. Invoicing and payment will almost always differ in time from the moment when the resources are *actually* consumed. Therefore, if AC is mistaken as financial cash flow, then false cost variances will be reported. For example, an up-front payment of materials acquired may generate an incorrect negative value in cost variance. Costs should only be reported as part of AC when resources are consumed as a consequence of being applied to scope accomplishment.

G.5.5 Estimating Actual Cost (AC) and Revising It Retrospectively

There are real-life situations where the data and information required to determine actual costs is not available at the end of the control period. This can be due to various reasons, such as time delays in data collection, or in accruing indirect costs. These constraints will generate a delay in updating AC, where it could be behind the update of EV and thereby generate incorrect cost variance. In these situations, the value of AC for the time period can be estimated using various methods such as trend analysis, correlation, parametric models, or other approaches. When the data and information required becomes available at a later period, the AC value can be corrected retrospectively. These procedures to estimate and retrospectively update AC should be defined and established in the EVM system during planning to ensure traceability through the proper implementation of a log.

G.6 Inappropriate Assessment of the Earned Value During Work Execution

The earned value measures the work accomplished in the form of the value in the baseline budget (PMB) of the work accomplished to date, whether it is on time, ahead, or behind schedule. Besides the selection of the appropriate method to credit EV, there are situations where an incorrect assessment of earned value may take place, which may lead to incorrect variances and performance measures.

G.6.1 Scope Reduction: Cancellation of a WBS Package After EV Has Been Credited

When scope reduction occurs, there may be situations where the work packages being cancelled already have progress reported and therefore EV credited. In this scenario, a rebaseline will take place where the budget corresponding to the remaining work in the work packages that are being cancelled (BAC − EV) needs to be removed from the total budget of the work packages prior to their closure. If the scope associated with the cancellation remains on the project, but is not distributed to control accounts, then it should reside in undistributed budget until a final decision is made to remove it from the project.

G.6.2 Overestimation of Earned Value

There may be situations where the degree of physical accomplishment in a work package is overestimated. A typical example is the discovery of unexpected rework or errors in data collection and progress measurement. When these situations occur, depending on the causes and on the organizational procedures, a corrective action is required to eliminate or compensate for the incorrect variance. For example, in some environments, procedures do not allow for revising past reported EV information; therefore, reporting a negative value for EV in the next time period will be required (i.e. to reduce the cumulative EV). On the other hand, in other environments, past EV information can be changed and corrected so that an accurate and true representation of how the work actually progressed over time is produced (and for the benefit of the current project, and for a better benchmarking in future projects). Whatever procedure is adopted, it must be defined and established upfront in the EVM system during planning.

G.6.3 Inaccurate Measurement of Work Accomplished to Credit EV

Crediting EV is primarily based on measuring the amount of work accomplished in a work package. If this measurement is subjective and not sufficiently accurate and precise, incorrect performance measures may be produced and stakeholders could lose confidence in the use of EVM.

In addition to selecting a method to credit EV, proper and feasible data collection and metrics generation procedures need to be planned and implemented, to ensure that the measurement of the work accomplished is accurate and delivers sufficient precision. These procedures should also be timely, and the cost of implementing them should correspond with the project budget and importance. The process of measuring the work accomplished should be objectively auditable—this is essential for transparency and to ensure the stakeholders' confidence in EVM reporting.

G.7 Data Consistency Issues

The EVM method deals with data that integrates scope, cost, resources, and schedule. This multi-dimensional integration of the project data is prone to generate various forms of inconsistency. Some typical examples are as follows:

- *Incomplete work packages scheduled in the past.* The corresponding activities of the work not yet accomplished need to be scheduled in the future.

- *Remaining planned resources and budget in work packages scheduled in the past.* This will underestimate the required future resources. Resources and budget not yet consumed needs to be allocated to the work scheduled in the future.

- *Completed work packages with the completion date in the future.* Completed work needs to be scheduled in the past.

- *EV credited to work packages scheduled to be executed in the future.* Work is only accomplished in the past.

These and many other situations lead to the generation of incorrect EVM performance and variance measures by portraying an overall incorrect image of the project status. This will undermine the required confidence of stakeholders in the EVM method and will misguide management decisions. Therefore, some form of data quality controls must be put in place and planned as part of the EVM system, during project planning.

G.8 Inappropriate Consideration of Risk Management

Risk management is not optional in project management. Therefore, the risk process must be properly integrated into project planning and controlling, and this must be taken into account in the EVM system. The time and budget under the control of the project manager should incorporate the contingency reserves established by the risk process as part of responding to risks. Even with the most proactive risk management policies, there should always be some level of contingency reserves as a result of active acceptance and contingency plans. Contingency reserves are the project manager's responsibility and therefore proper budgeting and scheduling should be incorporated into the PMB.

There are various forms of considering and incorporating contingency reserves into the PMB. Whatever the method used, it must preserve the validity of the EVM metrics and performance measures. For example, if reserves are simply "diluted," or hidden, across the work packages, then the EVM performance measures in some cases will overestimate performance (where actual risk lower) and in other cases will underestimate (where actual risk is higher).

Contingency reserves should be allocated to the time period and work packages in which the corresponding risks were identified to possibly occur. When reserve is transferred from a reserve into to a work package to accommodate a contingency plan or a reaction to a risk that was simply accepted, the PMB must be revised to portray the new expected distribution of the work and cost over time.

G.9 Inappropriate Modeling of Subcontracted Work

Subcontracted work is executed by an external party. The planning and monitoring of this type of work from a buyer's perspective is different from the contractor's perspective. For example, the selling price for the contractor is the budgeted cost for the buyer, and the actual cost for the contractor might be visible under the contract for the buyer. Another example is the impact of rework; this could be extra cost for the contractor (AC) and a slowing down of EV for the buyer, or it could be extra cost for the buyer (AC) and a re-baseline (PMB) for the contractor. This will depend on who is responsible for the extra work required and on the type of contract.

It is important to note that, potentially, there can be two separate EVM systems: one that measures the internal performance of the contractor and another that measures the performance of the contracted work under the buyer's perspective as part of its own EVM system. Performance measures will often differ in both systems, especially cost performance. When modeling subcontracted effort in an EVM system, care must be taken not to confuse the two performance systems. The perspective to be considered is always the buyer's perspective.

Furthermore, in order to measure the performance of subcontracted work, the type of contract and the agreements about data collection established with the contractor are important factors to take into account. For example, in a fixed-price contract, unless there is no extra scope, rework, or other extra costs as part of the buyers responsibility, the AC is equal to the credited EV for the subcontracted work package. The measurement of work progress to credit EV is based on the data collected under contractual agreements. However, with a cost-reimbursable contract that has an incentive fee (CPIF), the method for determining the incentive fee needs to be accounted for in the PMB.

G.10 Inappropriate Use of the Base EVM Formulas in "Boundary" Conditions

The EVM method considers a number of metrics that can produce strange results if applied to extreme boundary conditions. In particular this is the case of ratios like SPI (EV/PV) and divisions like IEAC (BAC/CPI). For example, consider the case of SPI in Table G1:

Table G1. SPI Behavior

SPI = EV/PV	PV = 0	PV > 0
EV = 0	SPI = 0/0 = ? *No performance*	SPI = 0/PV = 0 *A late start*
EV > 0	SPI = EV/0 = ? *An early start*	SPI = EV/PV > 0 *Normal scenario*

The behavior of the SPI indicator in extreme conditions has been the basis of some controversy with regard to its use for the effective measurement of time performance, because it always floats to the value of 1 when the work is completed and/or the baseline completion date is reached. Alternatives have been proposed, for example, the use of the earned schedule concept (discussed in Appendix D), or a modified version of the SPI indicator based on work volume.[1]

Another example and simpler scenario is where CPI = EV/AC = 0, where EV = 0 (i.e., no work done) and AC>0 (i.e., cost has been incurred). In this case, IEAC = BAC/CPI = BAC / 0 = $+\infty$. In this case, a better forecast would be: IEAC = AC + BAC. The diagnosis of the cause is essential.

Extreme boundary conditions are identified and resolved under the specific circumstances where the project work is being executed. If not properly identified and resolved, this can lead to a lack of trust in the EVM system and even rejection.

G.11 Inappropriate Use of EVM for Forecasting Cost and Schedule

The term "forecast" has been used in the early days of the EVM method, primarily referring to trend analysis of cost and schedule.

For example, for an initial budget of BAC = $10,000, and where the CPI = 0.5 (i.e., $0.5 produced per each $1 spent), then the "at completion forecast" would be: IEAC = BAC / CPI = $10 000/0.5 = $20,000. Or in other words, the project cost will double.

This method of forecasts for both cost and schedule is often rejected as it often presents large variances at completion that may appear both exaggerated and unstable as the project progresses.

In fact, this type of forecast is really a trend that should be correctly read as: "...*if the performance of the project is not improved (i.e., through management intervention) and continues like this, the final cost of the project is likely to double.*"

The primary purpose is to deliver a warning about the consequences of the project past performance "propagating" into the future, and therefore these forecasts are a stimulus for management intervention. In other words, if the cause of past performance is not addressed and properly handled, the future performance will be like the past or even worse. Therefore, act!

Of course, as the project unfolds and performance changes, so does the forecast as it continually projects a new view of the project's future that is consistent with the most recent performance.

---

[1] Rodrigues, A. (2010). Effective measurement of time performance using earned value management—A proposed modified version for SPI tested across various industries and project types. *PM WORLD TODAY*, Monthly Column—OCTOBER 2010, Advances in Project Management. Available from *http://www.pmforum.org//library/column/2010/PDFs/oct/Column-RODRIGUES.pdf*

These forecasts based on trends analysis, are often misinterpreted as an attempt of the EVM method to *predict the inevitable future*—as if the future would not be affected by management responses. This is a misconception, since a project is a social system and not an independent physical system as one observes in the natural sciences. In social systems, forecasts have a strong influence in the future outcome since they trigger reaction.

G.12 Overreliance on the IT System/Software

While an IT system is essential to support integrated project planning and all the data collection required by the EVM method, whatever system is used should surrender to the needs and specific requirements of the project management process based on EVM.

Often overreliance on the IT system and/or software packaged limits the scope for interpreting the EVM metrics, criticizing results, and ultimately making good decisions.

The IT system helps management to develop a better image of the project but it does not deliver the ultimate image. To understand the status of the project, the project manager needs to understand the context of the data. EVM data is an indicator of project progress; however, it must be combined with analysis and critical thinking to understand the meaning and implications of the data.

G.13 Inappropriate Level of Disaggregation Leading to Excessive Data

Decomposing the project work into elementary subpackages helps in improving the accuracy of estimates, in establishing progress measurement metrics, and in assigning responsibilities. All of this is positive for the purpose of implementing the EVM method.

However, excessive decomposition can lead to serious problems in using EVM metrics. As the work is further decomposed into even more elementary work tasks, variation during execution tends to increase in those small work packages ultimately leading to "noise" or random and meaningless variation.

The EVM metrics are primarily cumulative and, therefore, some accumulation of results is important for variation to be meaningful and helpful in devising management responses.

Care should be taken not to decompose the work packages into excessive detail. Besides meaningless information, there is also a significant increase in the management overhead effort required to collect and maintain the EVM data.

G.14 Not Using EVM at the Portfolio and Program Management Levels

The EVM method was developed to measure scope accomplishment and cost and schedule performance. The term "earned value" actually relates to "scope accomplished."

However, the term "earned value" is often interpreted by managers to mean "realized benefits" or "produced economic value." In most cases for projects, the budget value of the scope accomplished does not equate to the value of business benefits achieved, nor economic value produced.

For that to be the case, EVM concepts would have to be applied at the program and portfolio level, to measure the performance of programs based on benefits realization and the performance of portfolios based on the creation of organizational values.[2]

---

[2] Rodrigues, A. (2012). Earned Value Management for Programmes and Portfolios. *Advances in Project Management Series*. London: Ashgate. Available from *http://www.gowerpublishing.com/default.aspx?page=637&calcTitle=1&title_id=10483&edition_id=13261*

GLOSSARY

Actual Cost (AC). The realized cost incurred for the work performed on an activity during a specific time period. This can be reported for cumulative to date or for a specific reporting period. Also known as actual cost of work performed (ACWP).

Actual Cost of Work Performed (ACWP). See *Actual Cost (AC).*

Actual Time (AT). The number of time periods from the start of the project to the project status date.

Apportioned Effort (AE). Effort applied to project work that is not readily divisible into discrete efforts for that work, but which is related in direct proportion to measurable discrete work efforts. The value for the apportioned effort is determined based on the earned value of the corresponding discrete activity.

Budget at Completion (BAC). The sum of all the budgets established for the work to be performed on a project, work breakdown structure component, control account, or work package. The project BAC is the sum of all work package BACs.

Budgeted Cost for Work Performed (BCWP). See *Earned Value (EV).*

Budgeted Cost for Work Scheduled (BCWS). See *Planned Value (PV).*

Contingency Reserve (CR). Budget within the performance management baseline that is allocated for identified risks that are accepted and for which contingent or mitigating responses are developed.

Control Account. A management control point where scope, budget, actual cost, and schedule are integrated and compared to earned value for performance measurement. Each control account may be further decomposed into work packages and/or planning packages. Control accounts can belong to only one WBS component and one organizational breakdown component.

Control Account Manager (CAM). The manager within the project's organizational breakdown structure (OBS) that has been given the authority and responsibility to manage one or more control accounts.

Cost Performance Index (CPI). A measure of the cost efficiency of budgeted resources expressed as the ratio of earned value to actual cost. It is the ratio of earned value (EV) to actual costs (AC). $CPI = EV/AC$. A value equal to or greater than one indicates a favorable condition and a value less than one indicates an unfavorable condition.

Cost Variance (CV). The amount of budget deficit or surplus at a given point in time. It is the difference between earned value (EV) and actual cost (AC). $CV = EV - AC$. A positive value indicates a favorable condition and a negative value indicates an unfavorable condition.

Discrete Effort. Work effort that can be planned and measured and that yields a specific output. Discrete effort is directly related to specific end products or services with distinct and measurable points, and outputs that result directly from the discrete effort.

Distributed Budget. The budget for project scope that has been identified to work breakdown structure (WBS) control accounts and also has an identified control account manager.

Earned Value (EV). The measure of the work performed, expressed in terms of the budget authorized for that work. Earned value can be reported for cumulative to date or for a specific reporting period. Also known as budgeted cost for work performed (BCWP).

Earned Schedule Measure (ES). The time duration where EV equals PV. It measures the scheduled work accomplished, expressed in the time based unit of measure being utilized (e.g., week, month). ES can be reported either cumulative to date or for a specified reporting period. ES (cumulative) is equal to C plus I where C is the number of PMB time periods for which EV is equal to or exceeds PV. When EV exceeds PV_c, I is the fractional amount of ES for the subsequent incremental PV period. I is equal to $(EV - PV_c)/(PV_{c+1} - PV_c)$.

Earned Schedule Method. A method for extracting time-based schedule information from EVM data.

Estimate at Completion (EAC). The expected total cost of completing all work expressed as the sum of the actual cost to date (AC) and the estimate to complete (ETC). EAC = AC + ETC.

Estimate at Completion (time) (EAC(t)). The expected total time of completing project work. EAC(t) is equal to the actual time (AT) plus the estimate to complete (time) (ETC(t)) for the remaining work. EAC(t) = AT + ETC(t).

Estimate to Complete (ETC). The estimated cost of completing the remaining work.

Estimate to Complete (time) (ETC(t)). The estimated duration of completing the remaining work.

Independent EAC. A mathematical or statistical approach to project an EAC or a range of EACs using EVM data. These EAC calculations are independent of any future project or environmental conditions, and are not a replacement for a derived (bottom-up) project EAC.

Independent EAC (time) (IEAC(t)). A mathematical or statistical approach to calculate a project duration or range of durations using EVM data. These IEAC(t) calculations are independent of any future project or environmental conditions, and are not a replacement for a derived (bottom-up) project completion date from the network schedule. Using earned schedule, the IEAC(t) is equal to the planned duration (PD) divided by SPI(t), referred to as the short-form formula, or the IEAC(t) is equal to actual time (AT) plus the planned duration of work remaining (PDWR) divided by a time-based performance factor (PF) or a combination of factors, referred to as the long-form formula.

Independent Estimate of the Completion Date (IECD). A mathematical or statistical approach to calculate a project completion date or range of completion dates using EVM data. These IECD calculations are independent of any future project or environmental conditions, and are not a replacement for a derived (bottom-up) project completion date from the network schedule. The IECD is equal to the project start date plus the IEAC(t).

Level of Effort (LOE). A method of measurement used for support-type activities which does not produce definitive end products that can be delivered or measured objectively. In this technique, earned value (EV) is measured by the passage of time.

Management Reserve (MR). An amount of the project budget base (PBB) withheld for management control purposes. These are budgets reserved for unforeseen work that is within scope of the project. The management reserve is not included in the performance measurement baseline (PMB).

Organizational Breakdown Structure (OBS). A hierarchical representation of the project organization that illustrates the relationship between project activities and the organizational units that will perform those activities.

Performance Measurement Baseline (PMB). An approved, integrated scope-schedule-cost plan for the project work against which project execution is compared to measure and manage performance. The PMB includes contingency reserve, but excludes management reserve.

Planned Duration (PD). The planned duration for the project.

Planned Duration of Work Remaining. The planned duration of the remaining work calculated using earned schedule. $PDWR = PD - ES$.

Planned Value (PV). The authorized budget assigned to scheduled work. Also known as budgeted cost for work scheduled (BCWS).

Planning Package (PP). Work and budget that have been identified to a control account but are not yet defined into work packages. This is a future effort for which detailed planning may not have been accomplished.

Project Budget Base (PBB). The total budget for the project, including any management reserve and estimated costs for work that has been authorized but is not yet fully defined. When the project is chartered by a contract, this is known as the contract budget base (CBB).

Responsibility Assignment Matrix (RAM). A structure that relates the project organizational breakdown structure to the work breakdown structure to help ensure that each component of the project's scope of work is assigned to a responsible person/team.

Schedule Performance Index (SPI). A meaure of schedule efficiency on a project. It is the ratio of earned value (EV) to planned value (PV). $SPI = EV/PV$. An SPI equal to or greater than one indicates a favorable condition and a value of less than one indicates an unfavorable condition.

Schedule Performance Index (time) (SPI(t)). A measure of time-based schedule efficiency on a project calculated using earned schedule. It is the ratio of earned schedule (ES) to actual time (AT). $SPI(t) = ES/AT$. An SPI(t) equal to or greater than one indicates a favorable condition and a value of less than one indicates an unfavorable condition. The SPI(t) will only revert to one at project completion if on time completion has been achieved.

Schedule Variance (SV). A measure of schedule performance on a project. It is the difference between the earned value (EV) and the planned value (PV). $SV = EV - PV$. An SV equal to or greater than zero indicates a favorable condition and a value of less than zero indicates an unfavorable condition.

Schedule Variance (time) (SV(t). A measure of schedule performance on a project calculated using earned schedule. It is the difference between the earned schedule (ES) and the actual time (AT). SV(t) is equal to ES minus AT. An SV(t) equal to or greater than zero indicates a favorable condition and a value of less than zero indicates an unfavorable condition. The SV(t) will only revert to zero at project completion if on-time completion has been achieved.

Summary Level Planning Budget (SLPB). A time-phased budget for far-term work that cannot be reasonably planned and allocated to control accounts. Also known as summary level planning packages (SLPPs).

To-Complete Performance Index (TCPI). A measure of the cost performance that must be achieved with the remaining resources in order to meet a specified management goal, such as the EAC or the BAC. For example: to-complete performance index = (remaining work)/(estimate to complete) = $(BAC - EV)/(EAC - AC)$.

To-Complete Schedule Performance Index (TSPI). The calculated projection of schedule performance that must be achieved on remaining work to meet a specified goal, such as the EAC(t) or the PD calculated using earned schedule. For example: to-complete schedule performance index = (remaining time)/(estimate to complete (time)) = $(PD - ES)/(EAC(t) - AT)$.

Undistributed Budget (UB). The budget for project scope that has not yet been identified to WBS elements and, below those, to control accounts. This budget has generally not been distributed to a responsible control account manager (CAM) and is not normally time-phased. Contingency reserve may also reside in UB.

Variance at Completion (VAC). A projection of the amount of budget deficit or surplus, expressed as the difference between the budget at completion (BAC) and the estimate at completion (EAC). $VAC = BAC - EAC$. It represents the amount of expected overrun or underrun.

Variance at Completion (time) (VAC(t)). The difference between the planned duration assigned to a project (PD) and the total estimate at completion (time) (EAC(t)). $VAC(t) = PD - EAC(t)$. It represents the amount of expected delay or early completion.

Variance Threshold. A predetermined range of normal outcomes that sets the acceptable performance boundaries within which the team practices management by exception. Generally established for cost, schedule, and at-completion variances (CV, SV, and VAC).

Work Breakdown Structure (WBS). A hierarchical decomposition of the total scope of work to be carried out by the project team to accomplish the project objectives and create the required deliverables.

Work Breakdown Structure Dictionary. A document that provides detailed deliverable, activity, and schedule information about each component in the work breakdown structure.

Work Package. The work defined at the lowest level of the work breakdown structure for which cost and duration can be estimated and managed. Each work package has a unique scope of work, budget, scheduled start and completion dates, and may only belong to one control account.

INDEX